SEVEN·STEP JOB SEARCH

cut your job search time in half

Second Edition

MICHAEL FARR

Also in JIST's Help in a Hurry Series

Same-Day Resume

Next-Day Job Interview

15-Minute Cover Letter

Overnight Career Choice

PART OF JIS

Works
America's Career Publisher

D1041711

SEVEN-STEP JOB SEARCH, SECOND EDITION

© 2006 by JIST Publishing, Inc.

Published by JIST Works, an imprint of JIST Publishing, Inc.
8902 Otis Avenue
Indianapolis, IN 46216-1033
Phone: 1-800-648-JIST   Fax: 1-800-JIST-FAX   E-mail: info@jist.com

Visit our Web site at **www.jist.com** for information on JIST, free job search tips, book chapters, and ordering instructions for our many products! For free information on 14,000 job titles, visit **www.careeroink.com**.

Previous edition titled *Seven Steps to Getting a Job Fast* (ISBN 1-56370-888-4).

See the back of this book for instructional materials appropriate for use with this book. Quantity discounts are available for JIST books. Please call our Sales Department at 1-800-648-5478 for a free catalog and more information.

Acquisitions and Development Editor: Lori Cates Hand
Contributing Editor: Rachel Singer Gordon
Interior Designer: Aleata Howard
Page Layout Coordinator: Carolyn J. Newland
Cover Designer: Katy Bodenmiller
Proofreader: Jeanne Clark
Indexer: Tina Trettin

Printed in the United States of America
10 09 08 07 06 05   9 8 7 6 5 4 3 2 1

Library of Congress Cataloging-in-Publication Data

Farr, J. Michael.
    Seven-step job search : cut your job search time in half / Michael Farr.—
    2nd ed.
        p. cm. — (JIST's help in a hurry series)
    Rev. ed. of: Seven steps to getting a job fast. 2002.
    Includes index.
    ISBN 1-59357-239-5 (alk. paper)
    1. Job hunting. 2. Résumés (Employment) 3. Employment interviewing.
    I. Farr, J. Michael. Seven steps to getting a job fast. II. Title. III. Series.
    HF5382.7.F377 2006
    650.14—dc22
                                    2005027209

We have been careful to provide accurate information in this book, but it is possible that errors and omissions have been introduced. Please consider this in making any career plans or other important decisions. Trust your own judgment above all else and in all things.

Trademarks: All brand names and product names used in this book are trade names, service marks, trademarks, or registered trademarks of their respective owners.

ISBN 1-59357-239-5

About This Book

Compared to many job search books, this is a short book. I set out to make it that way, by covering only those things I have found will make the most difference to you in getting a good job in less time.

You could read parts of this book in a morning and conduct a more effective job search that same afternoon. Completing the worksheets and other activities (such as writing a resume) would take more time, of course, but most people should be able to complete this book in a day or less. And you might find that this is all you need.

Although career planning and job search can become complicated, here are a few simple truths:

1. If you have to work, you might as well do work you enjoy doing and are good at.

2. If you are going to look for a job, you might as well use methods that are likely to reduce the time it takes to find one.

These are the things I emphasize in this book. Of course, there is more to know about career planning and job seeking, but this book covers the basics. If you use the techniques—and not just read about them—the odds are good that you will reduce the time it takes to find your next job. And you will be more likely to find a better job than you might have otherwise.

I wish you well.

Mike Farr

Acknowledgments

The more you give away, the more you get back in return…

I don't know where to begin thanking everyone who has helped me over the years, but here is a start:

My Mom: Born in 1908, and independent until her death in 2002, Anna continues to inspire me. She was personally responsible for rearranging my books face-out in bookstores throughout southwest Florida, should you ever wonder about that.

My Dad: He modeled the work ethic I have, and the persistence (there were five kids in the family…). He retired after 29 years with the same employer, a remarkable record by today's standards. Thanks for being there. Oh, I'm sorry for all the trouble I caused you as a teenager.…

Sister William Mary: My teacher in grades 5, 6, 7, and 8. She and others taught me how to write and think. Thanks for being a good teacher.

A.J. Nania: My freshman-year English professor at Notre Dame. He taught me to write things short and long and to understand eighth-grade grammar. Short is harder, I learned, and takes longer per page. A great teacher.

Sandra: We've been married more than 35 years now, and she's been there through all my career changes and most of my life. I still like spending time with her, can you imagine? Thanks for everything.

My family: I am blessed with two great adult children, two brothers, two sisters, aunts and uncles, nieces and nephews, and lots of cousins. Wish they all lived closer.

Everyone else: I have a very long list of people who have helped me along the way, including good friends, the good people I work with, the many job seekers from whom I have learned so much, and so many others.

Thanks.

Contents

A Brief Introduction to Using This Book 1

Step 1: Identify Your Key Skills—and Develop
a Powerful New "Skills Language" to
Describe Yourself 3

    Learn the Three Types of Skills..................................3

    Identify Your Skills 5

    Key Points: Step 1 12

Step 2: Set a Specific Job Objective Before You
Go Looking 13

    Define Your Ideal Job Now; You Can Always Compromise
        Later..13

    How to Explore Specific Job Titles and Industries 17

    Consider Self-Employment or Starting a Business
        as Options, Too 33

    And, Now, We Return to Job-Related Skills 34

    Key Points: Step 2 36

Step 3: Use the Most Effective Methods to Find
a Better Job in Less Time 37

    How Do People Look for Jobs?...................................37

    Get the Most Out of Less-Effective Job Search Methods 38

    The Two Job Search Methods That Work Best 42

    Use JIST Cards—A Mini-Resume and a Powerful Job
        Search Tool...49

    Tips for Using the Internet in Your Job Search 58

    Key Points: Step 3 62

Step 4: Write a Simple Resume Now and a Better
One Later 63

    Tips for Creating a Superior Resume 63

    The Five Most Effective Ways to Use a Resume 65

    Types of Resumes 66

    Write a Chronological Resume 68

    Writing Your Skills Resume 87

Electronic and Scannable Resumes 90

Effective Cover Letters 94

More Sample Resumes 99

Key Points: Step 4 109

Step 5: Redefine What Counts as an Interview, and Then Organize Your Time to Get Two a Day 111

Make Your Search a Full-Time Job 112

Decide How Much Time You Will Spend Looking for Work Each Week and Day 112

Create a Specific Daily Job Search Schedule 113

Key Points: Step 5 115

Step 6: Dramatically Improve Your Interviewing Skills 117

Eight Important Actions for Interview Success 118

The Three-Step Process for Answering Most Interview Questions 128

Negotiating Salary 131

Key Points: Step 6 137

Step 7: Follow Up on All Job Leads 139

Thank-You Notes Make a Difference 139

Develop an Organized System for Following Up 140

Key Points: Step 7 143

In Closing..144

Appendix A: The Essential Job Search Data Worksheet 145

Appendix B: Sample Job Description from the *Occupational Outlook Handbook* 155

Some Tips for Using the *OOH* Job Descriptions in Your Job Search 155

Sample Job Description from the *Occupational Outlook Handbook* 156

Appendix C: A Short List of Additional Resources 171

Index 175

A Brief Introduction to Using This Book

Why does it take some people more time than others to find a job? And what sort of job should you be looking for?

The answers to these questions will require you to learn something about career planning and job seeking. But you can't just read about getting a job. Job seeking requires action, and the most effective action is to go out and make contacts with the people who are most likely to need someone with your skills. And the best way to do *that* is to make a job out of getting a job.

This might sound simple, but doing it well requires some preparation. After many years of experience, I have identified just seven basic things that make a big difference in your job search. This book covers and expands upon each of them. These steps are the following:

1. **Identify your key skills.** Most people can't explain what they are good at or what they like to do. Spending some time to clarify this will help you in so many ways, in your job search and in your life.

2. **Set a specific job objective before you go looking.** Too many people look for *a* job without knowing what *the* job would be. So I encourage you to define your ideal position, knowing you can always compromise later.

3. **Use the most effective job search methods.** Once you know what you are looking for, you need to know which job search methods are most likely to help you find it. This book points out these methods for you and shows you the most effective ways to use them.

4. **Write a simple resume now and a better one later.** Most people spend too much time worrying about their resume. Instead, you will learn to write an acceptable resume in just an hour or so and then a better one later, if you need one.

5. **Organize your time to get two interviews a day.** Yes, it's possible to get two interviews a day—if you know how to do it, and if you redefine what counts as an interview.

6. **Dramatically improve your interviewing skills.** Just an hour or so spent reading this section of the book can make a big difference in how well you handle your next interview. What you learn could, indeed, increase your earnings a thousand dollars or more.

7. **Follow up on all job leads.** Doing this well often makes the difference between who gets the job and who continues to wait for an offer.

Of Course, You Can't Just Read About It

As I said earlier, to get results you will have to actively apply what you learn in this book. One of the biggest reasons some people stay unemployed longer than others do is that they sit at home waiting for someone to knock on their door, call them up, or make them an offer via e-mail. That passive approach too often results in their waiting and waiting, while others are out there getting the offers.

So, Trust Me—Do the Worksheets

I know you will resist completing the worksheets. But, trust me—they are worth your time. Doing them will give you a better sense of what you are good at, what you want to do, and how to go about doing it. Spending some time to learn career planning and job seeking methods will likely result in your getting more interviews. And you will present yourself better in those interviews. Is this worth giving up a night of TV? Yes, I think so.

The interesting thing is that, once you finish this book and its activities, you will have spent more time planning your career than most people do. And you will know more than the average job seeker about finding a job.

Why This Is a Short Book

I've taught job seeking skills for many years, and I've written longer and more detailed books than this one. Yet I have often been asked to tell some-one, in a few minutes or hours, the most important things they should do in their career planning or job search. Instructors and counselors also ask the same question because they have only a short time to spend with the folks they're trying to help.

I've thought about what is most important to know, if time is short. The seven topics covered in this book are the ones I think are the most impor-tant to know. This book is short enough that you can scan it in a morning and conduct a more effective job search that afternoon. Doing all the activ-ities will take more time but will prepare you far better. Of course, you can learn more about all of the topics *Seven-Step Job Search* covers, but this book might be all that you need.

Identify Your Key Skills— and Develop a Powerful New "Skills Language" to Describe Yourself

Knowing what you are good at is an essential part of doing well in a job interview, writing a good resume, and other pieces of the job search puzzle. It is also important in other ways. For example, unless you use the skills that you enjoy using and are good at, you are unlikely to be fully satisfied in your job.

Most people are not good at recognizing and listing the skills they have. I can tell you this based on many years of working with groups of job seekers. When asked, few people can quickly tell me what they are good at, and fewer still can quickly present the specific skills that are needed to succeed in the job they want.

Many employers also note that most job seekers don't present their skills effectively. According to one survey of employers, more than 90 percent of the people they interview cannot adequately define the skills they have that support their ability to do the job. They might have the necessary skills, but they can't communicate that fact. The information in this Step is designed to help you fix that problem.

Learn the Three Types of Skills

Simple skills such as closing your fingers to grip a pen (which is not simple at all if you consider the miracle of complex neuromuscular interactions that sophisticated robots can only approximate) are building blocks for more complex skills, such as writing a sentence, and even more complex skills, such as writing a book. Even though you have hundreds of skills, some will be more important to an employer than others. Some will be far more important to you in deciding what sort of job you want.

To simplify the task of skill identification, I have found it useful to think of skills in the three major categories: self-management skills, transferable skills, and job-related skills.

Self-Management Skills/Personality Traits

You probably take for granted the many skills you use every day to survive and function. I call these skills *self-management* or *adaptive skills* because they are the basic skills you need to manage and adapt to a variety of situations. Some of them could be considered part of your basic personality. Such skills, which are highly valued by employers, include getting to work on time, honesty, enthusiasm, and getting along with others.

Transferable Skills

Transferable skills are general skills that can be useful in a variety of jobs. For example, writing clearly, good language skills, or the ability to organize and prioritize tasks are desirable skills in many jobs. These skills are called *transferable skills* because they can be transferred from one job—or even one career—to another.

The Skills Employers Want

According to research from the U.S. Department of Labor and the American Association of Counseling and Development, most of the skills employers want are either self-management or transferable skills. Of course, specific job-related skills remain important, but basic skills form an essential foundation for success on the job. Here are the top skills employers identified:

1. The ability to learn new things

2. Basic academic skills in reading, writing, and computation

3. Good communication skills, including listening and speaking

4. Creative thinking and problem solving

5. Self-esteem, motivation, and goal setting

6. Personal and career development skills

7. Interpersonal/negotiation skills and teamwork

8. Organizational effectiveness and leadership

What is most interesting is that most of these skills are not formally taught in school. Yet these so-called "soft skills" are the ones that employers value most. Of course, job-related skills are also important (an accountant still needs to know accounting skills), but the self-management and transferable skills are the ones that allow you to succeed in any job.

If you have any weaknesses in one or more of the skills in the preceding list, consider improvements. In an interview, try to present your weaknesses as strengths. For example, if you don't have a specific skill that's required for a job, let the employer know that you don't, but add that you are eager to learn and you are a fast learner. This comment shows the employer that you are not afraid of learning new skills and that you are confident in your abilities. Furthermore, if you are already strong in one or more of the top skills employers want, look for opportunities to develop and use them in your work or to present them clearly in your resume and in interviews.

Job-Related Skills

Job-related skills are the skills people typically think of first when asked, "Do you have any skills?" They are related to a particular job or type of job. An auto mechanic, for example, needs to know how to tune engines and repair brakes. Other jobs require job-related skills in addition to the self-management and transferable skills needed to succeed in almost any job.

Identify Your Skills

Because being aware of your skills is so important in your job search, I include a series of checklists and other activities here to help you identify your key skills. Recognizing these skills is important so that you can select jobs that you will more likely enjoy and do well. Knowing your key skills—and having a good skills language—will also help you throughout your job search. A solid skills language will help you handle interviews more

> **Note:** *This system of dividing skills into three categories is not perfect. Some things, such as being trustworthy, dependable, or well-organized, are not skills as much as they are personality traits that cannot be acquired easily. There is also some overlap between the three skills categories. For example, a skill such as being organized might be considered either self-management or transferable. Even so, dividing skills into types makes it easier for most people to understand and define their skills.*

effectively, write better resumes, and find job openings that best match your skills. To begin identifying your skills, answer the question in the box that follows.

WHAT MAKES YOU A GOOD WORKER?

On the following lines, list three things about yourself that you think make you a good worker. Take your time. Think about what an employer might like about you or the way you work.

1._____

2._____

3._____

The skills you just wrote might be among the most important things that an employer will want to know about you. Most (but not all) people write self-management skills when asked this question. Whatever you wrote, these skills are often very important to mention in the interview and on your resume. In fact, presenting these skills well will often enable a less experienced job seeker to get the job over someone with better credentials. Most employers are willing to train a person who lacks some job-related skills but has the self-management skills that the employer is looking for. Some employers even prefer job seekers with better self-management skills than job-related skills because they are more flexible and not set in their ways.

Identify Your Self-Management Skills and Personality Traits

I have created a list of self-management skills that are important to employers. The ones listed as "The Minimum" are those that most employers consider essential for job survival, and many employers will not hire someone who has problems in these areas.

Look over the list and put a check mark next to each self-management skill that you possess. Put a second check mark next to those skills that are particularly important for you to use or include in your next job.

SELF-MANAGEMENT SKILLS WORKSHEET

The Minimum

____ Have good attendance	____ Meet deadlines
____ Am honest	____ Get along with supervisor
____ Arrive on time	____ Get along with coworkers
____ Follow instructions	____ Am hardworking, productive

Other Self-Management Skills

____ Coordinating	____ Intuitive	____ Problem-solving
____ Results-oriented	____ Decisive	____ Team player
____ Mentoring	____ Culturally tolerant	____ Multitasking
____ Friendly	____ Discreet	____ Patient
____ Ambitious	____ Quick-learning	____ Spontaneous
____ Good-natured	____ Eager	____ Persistent
____ Assertive	____ Loyal	____ Steady
____ Helpful	____ Efficient	____ Physically strong
____ Capable	____ Mature	____ Tactful
____ Humble	____ Energetic	____ Practical
____ Cheerful	____ Methodical	____ Proud of work
____ Imaginative	____ Enthusiastic	____ Competent
____ Modest	____ Reliable	____ Independent
____ Expressive	____ Tenacious	____ Well-organized
____ Motivated	____ Resourceful	____ Industrious
____ Flexible	____ Thrifty	____ Natural
____ Responsible	____ Conscientious	____ Formal
____ Trustworthy	____ Informal	____ Open-minded
____ Self-confident	____ Creative	____ Optimistic
____ Versatile	____ Intelligent	____ Sincere
____ Humorous	____ Dependable	____ Original

(continued)

(continued)

Other Self-Management Skills You Have

Add any self-management skills that were not listed but that you think are important to include.

_____

_____

_____

_____

_____

_____

Your Top Self-Management Skills

Carefully review the checklist you just completed and select the five self-management skills you feel are most important for you to tell an employer about or that you most want to use in your next job. These skills are *extremely* important to present to an employer in an interview.

1._____

2._____

3._____

4._____

5._____

Identify Your Transferable Skills

Over the years, I have assembled a list of transferable skills that are important in a wide variety of jobs. In the checklist that follows, the skills listed as "Key Transferable Skills" are those that I consider to be most important for success on the job. These skills are also those that are often required in jobs with more responsibility and higher pay, so you should emphasize these skills if you have them.

The remaining transferable skills are grouped into categories that might be helpful to you. Check each skill you are strong in, and then put a second check mark next to the skills you want to use in your next job. When you are finished, you should have checked 10 to 20 skills at least once.

TRANSFERABLE SKILLS CHECKLIST

Key Transferable Skills

____ Meeting deadlines	____ Solving problems
____ Planning	____ Managing money or budgets
____ Speaking in public	____ Managing people
____ Controlling budgets	____ Supervising others
____ Meeting the public	____ Increasing sales or efficiency
____ Negotiating	____ Accepting responsibility
____ Instructing others	____ Writing well
____ Organizing or managing projects	____ Computer and technology skills

Dealing with Data

____ Analyzing data or facts	____ Paying attention to detail
____ Negotiating	____ Locating answers or information
____ Investigating	
____ Comparing, inspecting, or recording facts	____ Synthesizing
	____ Calculating, computing
____ Auditing records	____ Evaluating
____ Counting, observing, compiling	____ Managing money
	____ Taking inventory
____ Keeping financial records	____ Classifying data
____ Researching	____ Using technology to analyze data
____ Budgeting	

(continued)

(continued)

Working with People

____ Administering	____ Being sensitive	____ Being tough
____ Being pleasant	____ Helping others	____ Understanding
____ Being diplomatic	____ Persuading	____ Interviewing others
____ Patient	____ Demonstrating	____ Listening
____ Counseling people	____ Being tactful	____ Being outgoing
____ Supervising	____ Confronting others	____ Being tolerant
____ Caring for others	____ Socializing	____ Trusting
	____ Having insight	____ Being kind
	____ Teaching	____ Negotiating

Using Words, Ideas

____ Being articulate	____ Editing
____ Corresponding with others	____ Writing clearly
____ Designing	____ Thinking logically
____ Inventing	____ Researching
____ Speaking in public	____ Being ingenious
____ Communicating verbally	____ Creating new ideas
____ Remembering information	

Leadership

____ Arranging social functions	____ Making decisions
____ Directing others	____ Getting results
____ Motivating people	____ Planning
____ Exercising self-control	____ Solving problems
____ Being competitive	____ Delegating
____ Explaining things to others	____ Mediating problems
____ Negotiating agreements	____ Running meetings
____ Motivating yourself	____ Taking risks

Creative, Artistic

---- Being artistic   ---- Performing, acting

---- Expressing yourself   ---- Appreciating music

---- Drawing   ---- Presenting artistic ideas

---- Dancing   ---- Playing instruments

Other Transferable Skills

---- Driving or operating vehicles

---- Assembling or making things

---- Building, observing, or inspecting things

---- Constructing or repairing buildings

Other Similar Transferable Skills You Have

Add any transferable skills that were not listed but that you think are important to include.

_____

_____

_____

_____

_____

_____

Your Top Transferable Skills

Select the five top transferable skills you have that you want to use in your next job and list them here.

1. _____

2. _____

3. _____

4. _____

5. _____

Identify Your Job-Related Skills

You can gain job-related skills in a variety of ways, including education, training, work, hobbies, or other life experiences. Many jobs require skills that are specific to that occupation. An airline pilot obviously needs to know how to fly an airplane; thankfully, having good self-management and transferable skills would not be enough to be considered for that job.

When you complete the Essential Job Search Data Worksheet in appendix A, keep in mind that you are looking for skills and accomplishments. Pay special attention to those experiences and accomplishments that you really enjoyed, because these experiences often demonstrate skills that you should try to use in your next job. When possible, quantify your activities or their results with numbers. Employers can relate more easily to percentages, raw numbers, and ratios than to quality terms such as *more, many, greater, less, fewer,* and so on. For example, saying "presented to groups as large as 200 people" has more impact than "did many presentations."

Key Points: Step 1

You have a variety of skills that you have acquired through various experiences, such as school and previous jobs. It's important to discover your top skills and emphasize them on your resume and in interviews. Your skills can be divided into three categories:

- **Self-management skills/personality traits:** the many skills you use every day to survive and function, such as honesty, punctuality, and enthusiasm.

- **Transferable skills:** general skills that can be useful in a variety of jobs, such as communication or organizational skills.

- **Job-related skills:** specific skills related to a particular job, such as tuning an engine or flying a plane.

Set a Specific Job Objective Before You Go Looking

Too many people look for a job without clearly knowing what they are looking for. So, before you go out looking for a job, you should first define exactly what you want—*the* job, not just *a* job.

Define Your Ideal Job Now; You Can Always Compromise Later

Most people think that a job objective is the same as a job title, but it isn't. You need to consider other elements of what makes a job satisfying for you. Then, later, you can decide what that job is called—its title—what industry it might be in, and what skills you need to do the job.

DESCRIBE YOUR CURRENT JOB OBJECTIVE IN GENERAL TERMS

In general terms, what sort of a job will you be looking for next? For example, if you are enrolled in a career education program, your next job will be related to your current training. Or your past work or other experience might give you a direction for your next job. In the space that follows, list one or more job titles and a brief description of the job you will look for next.

_____

_____

_____

_____

_____

Important Factors in Choosing Your Ideal Job

Let's take the general job description you wrote in the preceding worksheet and get more specific. The eight questions that follow will help you consider things that are important in defining a position that satisfies you fully. Once you have considered your answers, your task then becomes finding a position that is as close to your ideal job as possible.

1. **What skills do you want to use?**

   From the skills lists in Step 1 (pages 7–11), select the top five skills that you enjoy using and most want to use in your next job.

   _____

   _____

   _____

   _____

   _____

2. **What type of special knowledge do you have?**

   Perhaps you know how to fix radios, keep accounting records, or cook food. Write down the things you know from schooling, training, hobbies, family experiences, and other sources. One or more of these knowledge areas could make you a very special applicant in the right setting. _____

   _____

   _____

   _____

   _____

   _____

3. **With what types of people do you prefer to work?**

   Do you like to work with competitive people, or do you prefer hardworking folks, creative personalities, relaxed people, or some other types? _____

_____

_____

_____

_____

_____

4. **What type of work environment do you prefer?**

   Do you want to work inside, outside, in a quiet place, in a busy place, or in a clean place; or do you want to have a window with a nice view? List the types of environments that you would prefer most.

   _____

   _____

   _____

   _____

   _____

5. **Where do you want your next job to be located?**

   In what city or region? If you are open to living and working anywhere, what would your ideal community be like? Near a bus line? Close to a childcare center? Near your mom?

   _____

   _____

   _____

   _____

   _____

6. **How much money do you hope to make in your next job?**

   Many people will take less money if they like a job in other ways—or if they need to find a job quickly to survive. You should know the pay range of the general type of job you want next. Think about the minimum you would take as well as

(continued)

(continued)

what you would eventually like to earn. Your next job will probably pay somewhere in between. What benefits would you like to receive in addition to salary?

_____

_____

_____

_____

_____

7. **How much and what types of responsibility are you willing to accept?**

Usually, the more money you want to make, the more responsibility you must accept. Do you want to work by yourself, be part of a group, or be in charge? If you want to be in charge, how many people do you want to supervise?

_____

_____

_____

_____

_____

8. **What things are important or have meaning to you?**

Do you have important values you would prefer to include as a basis of the work you do? For example, some people want to help others, clean up the environment, build things, make machines work, gain power or prestige, or care for animals or plants. Think about what is important to you and how you might include this in your next job.

_____

_____

_____

_____

_____

Is It Possible to Find Your Ideal Job?

Can you find a job that meets all the criteria you just defined? Perhaps.
Some people do. The harder you look, the more likely you are to find it.
Although it is possible, you will likely need to compromise on some criteria, so it is useful to know what is *most* important to include in your next
job. Go back over your responses to the eight questions and mark those
few things that you would most like to have or include in your ideal job.
Then use the general job description you wrote at the beginning of this
Step to write a brief outline of this ideal job in the following box. Don't
worry about a specific job title, whether you have the experience, or other
practical matters yet.

THINGS MY IDEAL JOB SHOULD INCLUDE

_____

_____

_____

_____

_____

_____

How to Explore Specific Job Titles and Industries

You might find your ideal job in an occupation you haven't considered.
And, even if you are sure of the occupation you want, it might be in an
industry that you're not familiar with. This combination of occupation
and industry forms the basis for your job search, and you should explore a
variety of options.

Explore More Than 270 Specific Job Titles in the Occupational Outlook Handbook

Your ideal job has a variety of characteristics, but it does not yet have a job
title. The reason is that some of the things you want, such as a specific

work environment, can be found in many jobs and in many industries. But, to conduct an effective job search, it is helpful to limit your search to a range of jobs most likely to match your ideal job.

The most often used source of information on jobs is a book titled the *Occupational Outlook Handbook (OOH),* published by the U.S. Department of Labor. The list that follows presents more than 270 job titles from the *OOH,* covering 87% of the U.S. workforce.

You can simply find a job title that interests you and then get additional information on it from the *OOH.* The descriptions provide details on earnings, education or training required, skills and abilities needed, working conditions, related jobs, sources of additional information (including Internet sources), and other particulars.

Most libraries and bookstores have a copy of the *Occupational Outlook Handbook (OOH)* or of another book with the same information, titled *Top 300 Careers.* You can also read *OOH* job descriptions on the Internet at www.CareerOINK.com or at www.bls.gov/oco/home.htm.

> **Note:** *A sample job description from the* Occupational Outlook Handbook, *along with tips for using it, is included in appendix B.*

The *OOH* job titles in this list are arranged in clusters of related jobs. Major job groupings are centered, and any subgroupings are indicated in *bold* type. Job titles within the groupings are in plain type.

As you review the job titles in this list, put a check mark by those that most closely match your general job description or that would require similar skills. Then read about these jobs in the *OOH.*

OOH Job Titles

Management and Business and Financial Operations Occupations

Management Occupations

Administrative services managers

Advertising, marketing, promotions, public relations, and sales managers

Computer and information systems managers

Construction managers

Education administrators

Engineering and natural sciences managers

Farmers, ranchers, and agricultural managers

Financial managers

Food service managers

Funeral directors

Human resources, training, and labor relations managers and specialists

Industrial production managers

Lodging managers

Medical and health services managers

Property, real estate, and community association managers

Purchasing managers, buyers, and purchasing agents

Top executives

Business and Financial Operations Occupations

Accountants and auditors

Budget analysts

Claims adjusters, appraisers, examiners, and investigators

Cost estimators

Financial analysts and personal financial advisors

Insurance underwriters

Loan counselors and officers

Management analysts

Tax examiners, collectors, and revenue agents

Professional and Related Occupations

Computer and Mathematical Occupations

Actuaries

Computer programmers

(continued)

(continued)

Computer software engineers

Computer support specialists and systems administrators

Computer systems analysts, database administrators, and computer scientists

Mathematicians

Operations research analysts

Statisticians

Architects, Surveyors, and Cartographers

Architects, except landscape and naval

Landscape architects

Surveyors, cartographers, photogrammetrists, and surveying technicians

Engineers

Aerospace engineers

Agricultural engineers

Biomedical engineers

Chemical engineers

Civil engineers

Computer hardware engineers

Electrical and electronics engineers, except computer

Environmental engineers

Industrial engineers, including health and safety

Materials engineers

Mechanical engineers

Mining and geological engineers, including mining safety engineers

Nuclear engineers

Petroleum engineers

Drafters and Engineering Technicians

Drafters

Engineering technicians

Life Scientists

Agricultural and food scientists

Biological scientists

Conservation scientists and foresters

Medical scientists

Physical Scientists

Atmospheric scientists

Chemists and materials scientists

Environmental scientists and geoscientists

Physicists and astronomers

Social Scientists and Related Occupations

Economists

Market and survey researchers

Psychologists

Urban and regional planners

Social scientists, other

Science Technicians

Community and Social Services Occupations

Clergy

> Protestant ministers

> Rabbis

> Roman Catholic priests

Counselors

Probational officers and correctional treatment specialists

Social and human service assistants

Social workers

Legal Occupations

Court reporters

(continued)

(continued)

Judges, magistrates, and other judicial workers

Lawyers

Paralegals and legal assistants

Education, Training, Library, and Museum Occupations

Archivists, curators, and museum technicians

Instructional coordinators

Librarians

Library technicians

Teacher assistants

Teachers—adult literacy and remedial and self-enrichment education

Teachers—postsecondary

Teachers—preschool, kindergarten, elementary, middle, and secondary

Teachers—special education

Art and Design Occupations

Artists and related workers

Designers

Entertainers and Performers, Sports and Related Occupations

Actors, producers, and directors

Athletes, coaches, umpires, and related workers

Dancers and choreographers

Musicians, singers, and related workers

Media and Communication-Related Occupations

Announcers

Broadcast and sound engineering technicians and radio operators

Interpreters and translators

News analysts, reporters, and correspondents

Photographers

Public relations specialists

Television, video, and motion picture camera operators and editors

Writers and editors

Health Diagnosing and Treating Practitioners

Audiologists

Chiropractors

Dentists

Dietitians and nutritionists

Occupational therapists

Optometrists

Pharmacists

Physical therapists

Physician assistants

Physicians and surgeons

Podiatrists

Recreational therapists

Registered nurses

Respiratory therapists

Speech-language pathologists

Veterinarians

Health Technologists and Technicians

Cardiovascular technologists and technicians

Clinical laboratory technologists and technicians

Dental hygienists

Diagnostic medical sonographers

Emergency medical technicians and paramedics

Licensed practical and licensed vocational nurses

Medical records and health information technicians

(continued)

(continued)

Nuclear medicine technologists

Occupational health and safety specialists and technicians

Opticians, dispensing

Pharmacy technicians

Radiologic technologists and technicians

Surgical technologists

Veterinary technologists and technicians

Service Occupations

Healthcare Support Occupations

Dental assistants

Medical assistants

Medical transcriptionists

Nursing, psychiatric, and home health aides

Occupational therapist assistants and aides

Pharmacy aides

Physical therapist assistants and aides

Protective Service Occupations

Correctional officers

Firefighting occupations

Police and detectives

Private detectives and investigators

Security guards and gaming surveillance officers

Food Preparation and Serving Related Occupations

Chefs, cooks, and food preparation workers

Food and beverage serving and related workers

Building and Grounds Cleaning and Maintenance Occupations

Building cleaning workers

Grounds maintenance workers

Pest control workers

Personal Care and Service Occupations

Animal care and service workers

Barbers, cosmetologists, and other personal appearance workers

Childcare workers

Flight attendants

Gaming services occupations

Personal and home care aides

Recreation and fitness workers

Sales and Related Occupations

Cashiers

Counter and rental clerks

Demonstrators, product promoters, and models

Insurance sales agents

Real estate brokers and sales agents

Retail salespersons

Sales engineers

Sales representatives, wholesale and manufacturing

Sales worker supervisors

Securities, commodities, and financial services sales agents

Travel agents

Office and Administrative Support Occupations

Communications equipment operators

Computer operators

Customer service representatives

Data entry and information processing workers

(continued)

(continued)

Desktop publishers

Financial clerks

    Bill and account collectors

    Billing and posting clerks and machine operators

    Bookkeeping, accounting, and auditing clerks

    Gaming cage workers

    Payroll and timekeeping clerks

    Procurement clerks

    Tellers

Information and record clerks

    Brokerage clerks

    Credit authorizers, checkers, and clerks

    File clerks

    Hotel, motel, and resort desk clerks

    Human resources assistants, except payroll and timekeeping

    Interviewers

    Library assistants, clerical

    Order clerks

    Receptionists and information clerks

    Reservation and transportation ticket agents and travel clerks

Material-recording, -scheduling, -dispatching, and -distributing occupations

    Cargo and freight agents

    Couriers and messengers

    Dispatchers

    Meter readers, utilities

    Production, planning, and expediting clerks

    Shipping, receiving, and traffic clerks

Stock clerks and order fillers

Weighers, measurers, checkers, and samplers, recordkeeping

Office and administrative support worker supervisors and managers

Office clerks, general

Postal service workers

Secretaries and administrative assistants

Farming, Fishing, and Forestry Occupations

Agricultural workers

Fishers and fishing vessel operators

Forest, conservation, and logging workers

Construction Trades and Related Workers

Boilermakers

Brickmasons, blockmasons, and stonemasons

Carpenters

Carpet, floor, and tile installers and finishers

Cement masons, concrete finishers, segmental pavers, and terrazzo workers

Construction and building inspectors

Construction equipment operators

Construction laborers

Drywall installers, ceiling tile installers, and tapers

Electricians

Elevator installers and repairers

Glaziers

Hazardous materials removal workers

Insulation workers

Painters and paperhangers

Pipelayers, plumbers, pipefitters, and steamfitters

(continued)

(continued)

Plasterers and stucco masons

Roofers

Sheet metal workers

Structural and reinforcing iron and metal workers

Installation, Maintenance, and Repair Occupations

Electrical and Electronic Equipment Mechanics, Installers, and Repairers

Computer, automated teller, and office machine repairers

Electrical and electronics installers and repairers

Electronic home entertainment equipment installers and repairers

Radio and telecommunications equipment installers and repairers

Vehicle and Mobile Equipment Mechanics, Installers, and Repairers

Aircraft and avionics equipment mechanics and service technicians

Automotive body and related repairers

Automotive service technicians and mechanics

Diesel service technicians and mechanics

Heavy vehicle and mobile equipment service technicians and mechanics

Small engine mechanics

Other Installation, Maintenance, and Repair Occupations

Coin, vending, and amusement machine servicers and repairers

Heating, air-conditioning, and refrigeration mechanics and installers

Home appliance repairers

Industrial machinery installation, repair, and maintenance workers, except millwrights

Line installers and repairers

Maintenance and repair workers, general

Millwrights

Precision instrument and equipment repairers

Production Occupations

Assemblers and Fabricators

Food Processing Occupations

Metal Workers and Plastic Workers

Computer-control programmers and operators

Machinists

Machine setters, operators, and tenders—metal and plastic

Tool and die makers

Welding, soldering, and brazing workers

Printing Occupations

Bookbinders and bindery workers

Prepress technicians and workers

Printing machine operators

Textile, Apparel, and Furnishings Occupations

Woodworkers

Plant and System Operators

Power plant operators, distributors, and dispatchers

Stationary engineers and boiler operators

Water and liquid waste treatment plant and system operators

Other Production Occupations

Dental laboratory technicians

Inspectors, testers, sorters, samplers, and weighers

Jewelers and precious stone and metal workers

Ophthalmic laboratory technicians

Painting and coating workers, except construction and maintenance

Photographic process workers and processing machine operators

Semiconductor processors

(continued)

(continued)

Transportation and Material Moving Occupations

Air Transportation Occupations

Aircraft pilots and flight engineers

Air traffic controllers

Motor Vehicle Operators

Bus drivers

Taxi drivers and chauffeurs

Truck drivers and driver/sales workers

Rail Transportation Occupations

Water Transportation Occupations

Material Moving Occupations

Job Opportunities in the Armed Forces

Explore Specific Industries

The industry you work in can often be just as important as the occupation you select. For example, if you are looking for a position using your accounting skills but have always had an interest in the medical field, why not consider looking for an accounting-related job in the medical industry? Some industries will simply be more interesting to you than others, so focus your job search in those industries.

Another good reason to consider various industries is that some are likely to pay more than others do, often for the same skills or jobs. So, if the industry where you apply your skills is not that important to you, why not look in an industry that tends to pay better?

A book titled *40 Best Fields for Your Career* contains very helpful reviews for each of the major industries mentioned in the following list. Put a check mark by industries that interest you, and then learn more about the opportunities they present. Many libraries and bookstores carry this book, as well as the U.S. Department of Labor's *Career Guide to Industries,* or you can find the information on the Internet at www.CareerOINK.com or at www.bls.gov/oco/cg/.

MAJOR INDUSTRIES

Goods-Producing Industries

Agriculture, Mining, and Construction

Agriculture, forestry, and fishing

Construction

Mining

Oil and gas extraction

Manufacturing

Aerospace product and parts manufacturing

Apparel manufacturing

Chemical manufacturing, except pharmaceutical and medicine manufacturing

Computer and electronic product manufacturing

Food manufacturing

Motor vehicle and parts manufacturing

Pharmaceutical and medicine manufacturing

Printing

Steel manufacturing

Textile mills and products

Service-Producing Industries

Trade

Automobile dealers

Clothing, accessory, and general merchandise stores

Grocery stores

Wholesale trade

Transportation and utilities

Air transportation

Truck transportation and warehousing

(continued)

(continued)

Utilities

Information

Broadcasting

Motion picture and video industries

Publishing, except software

Software publishers

Telecommunications

Financial Activities

Banking

Insurance

Securities, commodities, and other investments

Professional and Business Services

Advertising and public relations services

Computer systems design and related services

Employment services

Management, scientific, and technical consulting services

Education and Health Services

Child daycare services

Educational services

Health services

Social assistance, except child daycare

Government

Federal government, excluding the Postal Service

State and local government, excluding education and hospitals

---

YOUR TOP JOBS AND INDUSTRIES WORKSHEET

Go back over your lists of job titles and industries. In the first item below, list the jobs that interest you most. Then select the industries that interest you most and list them in the second space.

These are the jobs and industries you should research most carefully. Your ideal job is likely to be found in some combination of these jobs and industries, or in more specialized but related jobs and industries.

The Five Job Titles That Interest You Most

_____

_____

_____

_____

_____

The Industries That Interest You Most

_____

_____

_____

_____

_____

Consider Self-Employment or Starting a Business as Options, Too

More than one in 10 workers are self-employed or own their own business. If these options interest you, consider them as well. Talk to people in similar roles to gather information and look for books and Web sites that provide information on options that are similar to those that interest you. The government's Small Business Administration site at www.sba.gov is one Web site to check out.

SELF-EMPLOYMENT AREAS OF INTEREST

In the following space, write your current interest in self-employment or starting a business in an area related to your general job objective.

_____

_____

_____

_____

_____

And, Now, We Return to Job-Related Skills

In Step 1, you identified the job-related skills you have gained from a variety of sources. These are the job-related skills to emphasize in interviews and on your resume.

Now it is time to review the jobs that most interest you and list the key skills you have to support each one. The skills lists you did in Step 1 will help you identify key skills. In addition, read the *OOH* descriptions for the jobs that interest you and identify key skills each job includes. The worksheets and sample *OOH* job description in the appendices will help you in this process.

THE TOP FIVE SKILLS MY IDEAL JOBS REQUIRE

Ideal Job #1: _____

Job-related skills it requires:

1. _____

2. _____

3. _____

4. _____

5. _____

Ideal Job #2:_____

Job-related skills it requires:

    1._____

    2._____

    3._____

    4._____

    5._____

Ideal Job #3:_____

Job-related skills it requires:

    1._____

    2._____

    3._____

    4._____

    5._____

Ideal Job #4:_____

Job-related skills it requires:

    1._____

    2._____

    3._____

    4._____

    5._____

Ideal Job #5:_____

Job-related skills it requires:

    1._____

    2._____

    3._____

    4._____

    5._____

Key Points: Step 2

- Defining your ideal job involves many things besides a job title: the skills you want to use in the job, special knowledge you have, types of people you prefer to work with, work environment you prefer, where you want the job to be located, how much money you want to make, the amount of responsibility you want, your personal values, and other considerations.

- You can find details on more than 270 major jobs in the *Occupational Outlook Handbook.*

- After you determine the jobs you want, you can explore the different industries where they can be found.

Use the Most Effective Methods to Find a Better Job in Less Time

Employer surveys have found that most employers don't advertise their job openings. They most often hire people they already know, people who find out about the jobs through word of mouth, or people who happen to be in the right place at the right time. Although luck plays a part in finding job openings, you can use the tips in this Step to increase your "luck."

How Do People Look for Jobs?

Let's look at the job search methods that people use. The U.S. Department of Labor conducts a regular survey of unemployed people actively looking for work. Following are the results of their most recent findings.

Percentage of Unemployed People Who Use Various Job Search Methods

- Contacted employer directly: 62.7%
- Sent out resumes/filled out applications: 54.5%
- Contacted public employment agency: 19.9%
- Placed or answered ads: 16.4%
- Contacted friends or relatives: 18%
- Contacted private employment agency: 7.7%
- Used other active search methods: 11.8%

Source: U.S. Department of Labor, Current Population Survey

The survey shows that most people use more than one job search technique. For example, one person might read want ads, fill out applications, and ask friends for job leads. Others might send out resumes, contact everyone they know through previous jobs, and sign up at employment agencies.

But the survey covered only seven job search methods and asked only whether the job seeker did or did not use each method. The survey did not cover Internet job searches, nor did it ask whether a method actually worked in getting job offers. Unfortunately, there hasn't been much conclusive recent research on the effectiveness of various job search methods. Most of what we know is based on older research and the observations of people who work directly with job seekers, such as professional resume writers and career counselors.

Get the Most Out of Less-Effective Job Search Methods

The truth is that every job search method works for someone. But experience and research show that some methods are more effective than others. Your task in the job search is to spend more of your time using more effective methods—and increase the effectiveness of all the methods you use.

So let's start by looking at some traditional job search methods and how you can increase their effectiveness. Only about one-third of all job seekers get their jobs using one of these methods, but you should still consider using them to some extent in your search. Later in the Step we'll reveal the most effective methods, the ones you should devote the most time to in your search.

Newspaper and Internet Help-Wanted Ads

Most jobs are never advertised, and only about 16 percent of all people get their jobs through the want ads. Everyone who reads the paper knows about these openings, so competition is fierce for the few advertised jobs.

The Internet also lists many job openings. But, as happens with newspaper ads, enormous numbers of people view these postings. A full 53 percent of people who find jobs online make direct contact with employers via a company's Web site, and another 17 percent use targeted "niche" sites to locate positions. The rest use large national sites such as Careerbuilder.com or

Monster.com. Some people do get jobs through the bigger sites, so go ahead and apply. Just be sure to spend most of your time using more effective methods.

Filling Out Applications

Most employers require job seekers to complete an application form. Applications are designed to collect negative information, and employers use applications to screen people out. If, for example, your training or work history is not the best, you will often never get an interview, even if you can do the job.

Completing applications is a more effective approach for young and entry-level job seekers. The reason is that there is a shortage of workers for the relatively low-paying jobs that less-experienced job seekers typically seek. As a result, when trying to fill those positions, employers are more willing to accept a lack of experience or job skills.

Even so, you will get better results by filling out the application, if asked to do so, and then requesting an interview with the person in charge.

When you complete an application, make it neat and error-free, and do not include anything that could get you screened out. If necessary, leave a problem section blank. You can always explain the situation after you get an interview.

Employment Agencies

There are three types of employment agencies. One is operated by the government and is free. The others, private employment agencies and temp agencies, are run as for-profit businesses and charge a fee to either you or an employer. Here are the advantages and disadvantages of using each.

The Government Employment Service and One-Stop Centers

Each state has a network of local offices to pay unemployment compensation, provide job leads, and offer other services at no charge to you or to employers. The service's name varies by state. It may be called "Job Service," "Department of Labor," "Unemployment Office," "Workforce Development," or another name. Many of these offices are now also online, and some even require their users to sign up with a login and password to search for job leads and use other services on the Internet.

Many states also have One-Stop centers that provide employment counseling, reference books, computerized career information, job listings, and other resources. See www.servicelocator.org for a searchable database of One-Stop centers.

The Employment and Training Administration Web site at www.doleta.gov/uses gives information on the programs provided by the government employment service, plus links to other useful sites. Another site, America's Job Bank (www.ajb.dni.us), enables visitors to see all jobs that are listed with the government employment service and to search for jobs by region and other criteria.

The government employment service lists only 5 to 10 percent of the available openings nationally, and only about 6 percent of all job seekers get their jobs there. Even so, visit your local office early in your job search. Find out whether you qualify for unemployment compensation and learn more about its services. Look into it—the price is right.

Private Employment Agencies

Private employment agencies are businesses that charge a fee either to you or to the employer who hires you. Fees can be from less than one month's pay to 15 percent or more of your annual salary. You will often see these agencies' ads in the help-wanted section of the newspaper. Many have Web sites.

Be careful about using fee-based employment agencies. Recent research indicates that more people use and benefit from fee-based agencies than in the past. However, relatively few people who register with private agencies get a job through them.

If you use a private employment agency, ask for interviews with employers who will pay the agency's fee. Do not sign an exclusive agreement or be pressured into accepting a job. Also, be sure to continue to actively look for your own leads. You can find these agencies in the phone book's yellow pages, and many state-government Web sites offer lists of the private employment agencies in their states.

Temporary Agencies

Temporary agencies offer jobs that last from several days to many months. They charge the employer an hourly fee, and then pay you a bit less and keep the difference. You pay no direct fee to the agency. Many private employment agencies now provide temporary jobs as well.

Temp agencies have grown rapidly for good reason. They provide employers with short-term help, and employers often use them to find people they might want to hire later. If the employer doesn't think the temp worker does a good job, they can just ask the agency to send someone else.

> **Tip:** *Temp agencies can help you survive between jobs and get experience in different work settings. Temp jobs provide a very good option while you look for long-term work, and you might get a job offer while working as a temp. Holding a temporary job might even lead to a regular job with the same or a similar employer.*

School and Other Special Employment Services

Only a small percentage of job seekers use this option. This is probably because few have the service available to them. If you are a student or graduate, find out about these services at your school. Some schools provide free career counseling, resume-writing help, referrals to job openings, career interest tests, reference materials, Web sites listing job openings, and other services.

Special career programs work with veterans, people with disabilities, welfare recipients, union members, professional groups, and many others. Check out these services and consider using them.

Mailing Resumes and Posting Them on the Internet

Many job search "experts" used to suggest that sending out lots of resumes was a great technique. That advice probably helped sell their resume books, but mailing resumes to people you do not know was never an effective approach. It very rarely works. A recent survey of 1,500 successful job seekers showed that only 2 percent found their positions through sending an unsolicited resume.

Although mailing your resume to strangers doesn't make much sense, posting it on the Internet might because

- It doesn't take much time.

- Many employers have the potential of finding your resume there.

- You can post your resume on niche sites that attract only employers in your field.

- Your Internet resume is easily updated, allowing you to post your current accomplishments.

- You can easily "link" your resume to projects and Web sites that highlight your accomplishments.

Job searching on the Internet has its limitations, just like other methods do. You should stick with posting your resume online and using it to apply for appropriate positions. Just as blindly mailing your resume to employers has little chance of success, blindly e-mailing your resume to employers is an ineffective, and even counterproductive, strategy. E-mail makes it even easier to send out lots of resumes, and 63 percent of recruiters and hiring managers complain about being "blasted" with unsolicited resumes. This fails to make a good impression, and makes it harder for them to find good candidates.

> **Note:** *I cover electronic resumes in more detail in Step 4.*

The Two Job Search Methods That Work Best

The fact is that most jobs are not advertised. So how do *you* find them? The same way about two-thirds of all job seekers do—networking with people you know (which I call making *warm contacts*) and directly contacting employers (which I call making *cold contacts*). Both of these methods are based on the job search rule that you should know above all:

THE MOST IMPORTANT JOB SEARCH RULE:
DON'T WAIT UNTIL A JOB IS "OPEN" BEFORE YOU CONTACT
THE EMPLOYER!

Employers fill most jobs with people they meet before a job is formally "open." So, the trick is to meet people who can hire you before a job is formally available. Instead of asking, "Do you have any jobs open?" I suggest that you say, "I realize you may not have any openings now, but I would still like to talk to you about the possibility of future openings."

This simple change in how you approach the job search can make an enormous difference in your getting interviews while others wait for jobs to be advertised. They remain unemployed, while you get interviews and job offers. Here are some details on how to do this most effectively.

Most-Effective Job Search Method #1: Develop a Network of Contacts

Studies find that more than 60 percent of all people locate their jobs through a lead provided by a personal contact. That makes people you know the #1 source of job leads. Asking their help is more effective than all other job search methods.

Developing contacts is called *networking*, and here's how it works:

1. **Make lists of people you know.** Make a thorough list of anyone you are friendly with. Then make a separate list of all your relatives. These two lists alone often add up to 25 to 100 people or more. Next, think of other groups of people with whom you have something in common, such as former co-workers or classmates, members of your social or sports groups, members of your professional association, former employers, neighbors, and other groups. You might not know many of these people personally or well, but most will help you if you ask them.

> **Tip:** *It's true. You have to know someone to get a job. I have found, though, that you can quickly get to know all sorts of new people if you go about it right. One of them often turns out to be the someone you need.*

CREATE YOUR LISTS OF CONTACTS

Make a separate networking list for each group. Check any of the following groups that make sense for your situation.

- Friends

- Relatives

- Friends of parents

- Former co-workers

- Members of my church or religious group

- People who sell me things (insurance agent, real estate agent, landlord, and so on)

- Neighbors

(continued)

(continued)

- People I went to school with

- Former teachers

- Members of social clubs

- People who provide me with services (hair stylist, counselor, mechanic, and so on)

- Former employers

- Members of sports or hobby groups

- Members of professional organizations I belong to or can join

Write in other groups here:

_____

_____

_____

_____

Next, list names and contact information for each person in each group. It might take some research to collect all of the names and contact information, so start with lists of friends and relatives, whose information is easy to get. Some lists, like those from alumni associations or professional organizations, can also be obtained with a quick phone call or e-mail, or by searching a Web site.

2. **Contact them in a systematic way.** Contact each person on your lists. Obviously, some people will be more helpful than others, but any one of them might help you find a job lead.

3. **Present yourself well.** Begin with your friends and relatives. Call and tell them you are looking for a job and need their help. Be as clear as possible about the type of employment you want and the skills and qualifications you have. Look at the sample JIST Card and phone script later in this Step for good presentation ideas.

4. **Ask contacts for leads.** It is possible that your contacts will know of a job opening that interests you. If so, get the details and get right on it! More likely, however, they will not, so you should ask each person the Three Magic Networking Questions.

The Three Magic Networking Questions

- **Do you know of any openings for a person with my skills?** If the answer is "No" (which it usually is), ask...

- **Do you know of someone else who might know of such an opening?** If your contact does, get that name and ask for another one. If he or she doesn't, ask...

- **Do you know of anyone who might know of someone else who might know of a job opening?** Another good way to ask this is "Do you know someone who knows lots of people?" If all else fails, this will usually get you a name.

5. **Contact these referrals and ask them the same questions.** From each person you contact, try to get two names of other people you might contact. Doing this consistently can extend your network of acquaintances by hundreds of people. Eventually, one of these people will hire you or refer you to someone who will!

If you are persistent in following these five steps, networking might be the only job search method you need. It works.

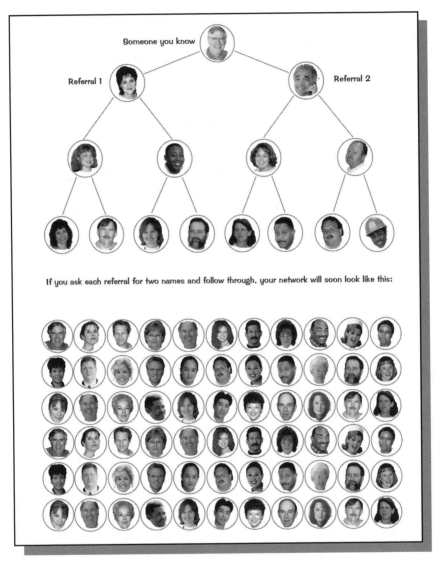

Figure 3-1: Networking in action.

Most-Effective Job Search Method #2: Contact Employers Directly

It takes more courage, but making direct contact with employers is a very effective job search technique. I call these *cold contacts* because people you don't know in advance will need to warm up to your inquiries. Two basic techniques for making cold contacts follow.

The Reason Most Jobs Are Not Advertised

Three out of four jobs are never advertised because employers don't need to advertise or don't want to. First of all, advertising a job opening takes time and money that many employers don't have. Also, employers trust people referred to them by someone they know far more than they trust someone selected from a group of unknown strangers. Most jobs are filled by referrals and people the employer knows. This eliminates the need to advertise. So your job search must involve more than looking at ads.

Use the Yellow Pages to Find Potential Employers

Begin by looking at the index in the front of your phone book's yellow pages. For each entry, ask yourself, "Would an organization of this kind need a person with my skills?" If you answer "Yes," that organization or business type is a possible target. You can also rate "Yes" entries based on your interests, writing a "1" next to those that seem very interesting, a "2" next to those that you are not sure of, and a "3" next to those that aren't interesting at all.

Here is one section of a yellow pages listing that has been marked by a person looking for a position in health care.

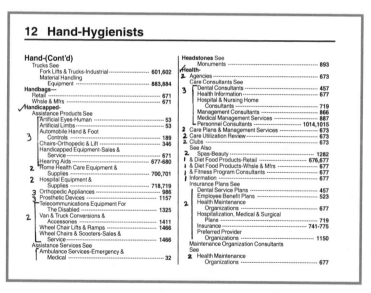

Figure 3-2: A yellow pages listing marked up by a job seeker.

Next, select a type of organization that got a "Yes" response and turn to that section of the yellow pages. Call each organization listed there and ask to speak to the person who is most likely to hire or supervise you. This would typically be the manager of the business, or a department head—not the personnel or human resources manager.

Once you have identified target employers, call them to find out whether they have any openings. Here is an example of a carefully scripted phone call made to the manager of a small business. You will learn more about how to create these later in this Step.

> **Note:** *You can easily adapt this approach to the Internet. Use sites such as www. yellowpages.com to get phone contacts anywhere in the world, or find phone and e-mail contacts on an employer's own Web sites.*

> *"Hello, my name is John Kijek. I am interested in a position as an auto mechanic. I have more than three years of experience, including one year in a full-time auto mechanic's training program. I am familiar with all hand tools and electronic diagnostic equipment, and can handle common auto-repair tasks, such as tune-ups, brakes, exhaust systems, and electrical and mechanical repairs. I also work quickly, often completing jobs correctly in less than the standard time. I have all the tools needed to start work immediately. I can work any shift and prefer full-time work. I am also honest, reliable, and good with people. When may I come in for an interview?"*

Drop In Without an Appointment

Another effective cold contact method is to just walk into a business or organization that interests you and ask to speak to the person in charge.

The Almost-Perfect Source of Free Contacts

Your phone book's yellow pages provide the most complete and up-to-date listing of potential job search targets you can get. It even organizes them into categories that are very useful for a job seeker. Just find a category that interests you, call each listing, and ask to speak with the person who is most able to hire or supervise someone with your skills.

Remember to say that you realize there might not be a job opening now, but that you would like to be considered for a future opening. If your timing is inconvenient, ask for a better time to come back for an interview.

Try this four or five times, and you will be surprised to find that you will often get one or two interviews this way.

Dropping in is particularly effective in small businesses, but it also works surprisingly well in larger ones. Look for drop-in opportunities on your way to or from another interview. It is an unconventional approach that can work very well, enabling you to see employers before they have an opening. And, if they like you and if you stay in touch, they are more likely to hire you than to advertise the opening.

Most Jobs Are with Small Employers

Businesses and organizations with fewer than 250 employees employ about 72 percent of all U.S. workers. Small businesses are also the source for around 75 percent of the new jobs created each year. They are simply too important to overlook in your job search! Many of them don't have personnel departments, which makes direct contacts even easier and more effective.

Use JIST Cards—A Mini-Resume and a Powerful Job Search Tool

JIST Cards are a job search tool that gets results. I first developed them many years ago, almost by accident. I helped job seekers create them to get attention and "leave something behind" after dropping in without appointments to ask for interviews with employers. Many thousands of job seekers have used them in every imaginable print and electronic format and they still get attention—and interviews—that more traditional tools do not.

Think of a JIST Card as a very small resume. A JIST Card is carefully constructed to contain all the essential information most employers want to know in a very short format. It typically uses a 3 × 5–inch card format, but has been designed into many other sizes and formats, such as a folded business card.

Your JIST Card can be as simple as handwritten or as complex as created on a computer with graphics and on special papers. You create a JIST Card in addition to a resume because a JIST Card is used in a different way.

JIST Cards Get Results

What matters is what JIST Cards accomplish—they get results. In our surveys of employers, more than 90 percent of people receiving JIST Cards form a positive impression of the writer within 30 seconds. More amazing is that about 80 percent of employers say they would be willing to interview the person behind the JIST Card, even if they did not have a job opening now.

How You Can Use Them

You can use a JIST Card in many ways, including the following:

- Attached to your resume or application
- Enclosed in a thank-you note
- Given to your friends, relatives, and other contacts—so they can give them to other people
- Sent out to everyone who graduated from your school or who are members of a professional association
- Put on car windshields
- Posted on the supermarket bulletin board
- In electronic form as an e-mail or e-mail attachment

I'm not kidding about finding JIST Cards on windshields or bulletin boards. They can be included on Web sites along with your resume or included as text or attachments in e-mail to people you know, with a request to forward it to others. We've seen them used in these ways and hear about more ways people are using them all the time.

JIST Cards are an effective job search tool! Give them to friends and network contacts. Attach one to a resume. Enclose them in your thank-you notes before or after an interview. Leave one with an employer as a business card. Send one as an e-mail or e-mail attachment for people to forward to others. Use them in many creative ways. Put lots of them into circulation and you might be surprised at how well they work.

Writing Your JIST Card

A JIST Card is small, so it can't contain many details. It should list only the information that is most important to employers. To write your card, follow these steps:

1. **Type your name at the top of the card.** You can center it and use bold text to make it stand out, as you would on a resume. Keep this simple and professional. Don't use nicknames, middle names, or initials.

2. **Give two ways for the employer to contact you.** Space down a few lines and left-align this information. Generally, all you will need to include is your daytime phone number or cell phone number (always include your area code) and your e-mail address.

3. **Give a broad job objective.** Space down another line or two and left-align this information. Don't be too narrow in your job objective. Say "General office" rather than "Receptionist" if you would consider a variety of office jobs. If you are narrower in your job objective, try to avoid a narrow job title and give other details. For example, say "Management position in an insurance-related business" or "Working with children in a medical or educational setting." Don't limit yourself to entry-level jobs if you have potential or interest in doing more. If you say "Office manager" instead of "Secretary," you just might get a more-responsible and higher-paying job. If you are not sure of your ability to get a higher-paying job, it is still best to keep your options open. Say "Office manager or responsible secretarial position," for example.

4. **List your years of experience.** Space down again and add one sentence that summarizes how long you have been working in this field. You should take advantage of all the experience you have that supports your job objective. Depending on your situation, you can include any or all of the following as part of your work experience: paid work, volunteer work, informal work, and related education and training.

   If you have lots of work experience, emphasize the experience that is closest to your job objective. For example, if you have 20 years of total experience, include just the experience that directly relates to this job. Say "More than 15 years of experience." This keeps the employer from knowing how old you are. Your age is an advantage that you will present in the interview!

   If you don't have much paid work experience, emphasize your education, training, and other work. For example, "Nearly two years of experience, including one year of advanced training in office procedures." Remember to include the total of all paid and unpaid work as part of your experience. Include all those part-time jobs and volunteer jobs by writing "More than 18 months of total work experience."

If your experience is in another field, mention that you have "Four years of work experience" without saying in what field.

Other points to emphasize: If you won promotions or raises, or have other special strengths, this is the time to say so. For example: "More than seven years of increasingly responsible work experience, including three years as a supervisor. Promoted twice."

5. **Detail your education and training.** In the same paragraph, add a sentence that tells what degrees, certifications, diplomas, and other relevant training you have. If it helps, you can combine your education and training with your experience on your JIST Card. Or you can list your education and training as a separate statement. Don't mention your education or training if it doesn't help you. If you have a license, certification, or degree that supports your job objective, mention it here. For example, "Four years of experience plus two years of training leading to certification as an Emergency Medical Technician."

6. **Showcase your job-related skills.** Still in the same paragraph, add up to four sentences that tell what you can do and how well you can do it. Be sure to include accomplishments and numbers to support them. For example, instead of writing "Can do word processing," say "Accurately word-process 80 words per minute and am familiar with advanced graphic and formatting capabilities of Microsoft Word and Quark." Add up the number of transactions you handled, the money you were responsible for, and the results you got. For example, a person with fast-food experience might write, "Have handled more than 50,000 customer contacts quickly and accurately with total sales of over $250,000." These numbers are based on a five-day work week, 200 customers a day for one year, and an average sale of $5. If appropriate, mention job-related tools or equipment you can use. Use the language of the job to describe the more important things you can do.

7. **State your availability and preferred working arrangements.** If applicable, space down and add a sentence that states any special availability you might have, such as "interested in part-time work," or "available with two weeks' notice." This is an optional section in which you can add just a few words to let the employer know what

you are willing to do. Do not limit your employment possibilities by saying "Will only work days" or "No travel wanted."

8. **End with your key adaptive skills.** Space down a few more lines and add one last sentence that tells what personality traits you have that make you a good employee (see Step 1 for help on determining these).

JIST Card Paper and Format Tips

Many office-supply stores have perforated light card-stock sheets to run through your computer printer. These will then tear apart into 3 × 5–inch cards. Many word-processing programs have templates that allow you to format a 3 × 5–inch card size. You can also use regular-size light card stock—available at office-supply stores—to print several cards on a sheet, and cut it to the size you need. Print shops can also photocopy or print them in the size you need. Get a few hundred at a time. They are cheap, and the point is to get lots of them in circulation.

Sample JIST Cards

The following sample JIST Cards use a plain format, but you can make them as fancy as you want. So be creative. Look over the examples to see how they are constructed. Some are for entry-level jobs and some are for more advanced ones.

Sandy Nolan

Position: General Office/Clerical

Message: (512) 232-9213

More than two years of work experience plus one year of training in office practices. Type 55 wpm, trained in word processing, post general ledger, have good interpersonal skills, and get along with most people. Can meet deadlines and handle pressure well.

Willing to work any hours.

Organized, honest, reliable, and hardworking.

Joyce Hua

Home: (214) 173-1659
Message: (214) 274-1436
Email: jhua@yahoo.com

Position: Programming/Systems Analyst

More than 10 years of combined education and experience in data processing and related fields. Competent programming in Visual Basic, C, C++, FORTRAN, and Java, and database management. Extensive PC network applications experience. Have supervised a staff as large as seven on special projects and have a record of meeting deadlines. Operations background in management, sales, and accounting.

Desire career-oriented position, will relocate.

Dedicated, self-starter, creative problem solver.

Paul Thomas

Home: (301) 681-3922
Message: (301) 681-6966
Cell phone: (301) 927-9856

Position: Research Chemist, Research Management
in a small-to-medium-sized company

Ph.D. in biochemistry plus more than 15 years of work experience. Developed and patented various processes with current commercial applications worth many millions of dollars. Experienced with all phases of lab work with an emphasis on chromatography, isolation, and purification of organic and biochemical compounds. Specialize in practical pharmaceutical and agricultural applications of chemical research. Have teaching, supervision, and project management experience.

Married more than 15 years, stable work history, results and task oriented, ambitious, and willing to relocate.

Richard Straightarrow **Home: (602) 253-9678**
Message: (602) 257-6643
E-mail: RSS@email.cmm

Objective: Electronics installation, maintenance, and sales

Four years of work experience plus a two-year A.S. degree in Electronics Engineering Technology. Managed a $360,000/year business while going to school full time, with grades in the top 25%. Familiar with all major electronic diagnostic and repair equipment. Hands-on experience with medical, consumer, communication, and industrial electronics equipment and applications. Good problem-solving and communication skills. Customer service oriented.

Willing to do what it takes to get the job done.

Self motivated, dependable, learn quickly.

Juanita Rodriguez   Message: (639) 361-1754
Email: jrodriguez@email.cmm

Position: Warehouse Management

Six years of experience plus two years of formal business course work. Have supervised a staff as large as 16 people and warehousing operations covering over two acres and valued at more than $14,000,000. Automated inventory operations resulting in a 30% increase in turnover and estimated annual savings more than $250,000. Working knowledge of accounting, computer systems, time and motion studies, and advanced inventory management systems.

Will work any hours.

Responsible, hardworking, and can solve problems.

Deborah Levy

Home: (213) 432-8064
Pager: (212) 876-9487

Position: Hotel Management Professional

Four years of experience in sales, catering, and accounting in a 300-room hotel. Associate degree in Hotel Management plus one year with the Boileau Culinary Institute. Doubled revenues from meetings and conferences. Increased dining room and bar revenues by 44%. Have been commended for improving staff productivity and courtesy. I approach my work with industry, imagination, and creative problem-solving skills.

Enthusiastic, well-organized, and detail-oriented.

Jonathan Michael

Cell phone: (614) 788-2434
E-mail: jonn@pike.org

Objective: Management

More than 7 years of management experience plus a B.S. degree in business. Managed budgets as large as $10 million. Experienced in cost control and reduction, cutting more than 20% of overhead while business increased more than 30%. Good organizer and problem solver. Excellent communication skills.

Prefer responsible position in a medium-to-large business.

Cope well with deadline pressure, seek challenge, flexible.

Use Your JIST Card as the Basis for an Effective Phone Script

The phone is an essential job search tool that can get you more interviews per hour than any other job search tool. But it won't work unless you use it actively throughout your search. Once you have created your JIST Card, you can use it as the basis for a phone "script" to make warm or cold calls. Revise your JIST Card content so that it sounds natural when spoken, and then edit it until you can read it out loud in about 30 seconds. The sample phone script that follows is based on the content of a JIST Card. Use it to help you modify your own JIST Card into a phone script.

> *"Hello, my name is Pam Nykanen. I am interested in a position in hotel management. I have four years of experience in sales, catering, and accounting with a 300-room hotel. I also have an associate degree in hotel management, plus one year of experience with the Brady Culinary Institute. During my employment, I helped double revenues from meetings and conferences and increased bar revenues by 46 percent. I have good problem-solving skills and am good with people. I am also well organized, hardworking, and detail oriented. When may I come in for an interview?"*

Once you have your script, make some practice calls to warm or cold contacts. If you're making cold calls, contact the person most likely to supervise you. Then present your script just as you practiced it, without stopping.

Although the sample script assumes that you are calling someone you don't know, you can change it to address warm contacts and referrals. Making cold calls takes courage but works very well for many who are willing to do it.

Note: *Making cold calls takes guts, but most people can get one or more interviews an hour using cold calls. Start by calling people you know and the people they refer you to. Then try calls to businesses that don't sound very interesting. As you get better, call more desirable targets. Hey, what's the worst that could happen?*

Tips for Using the Internet in Your Job Search

The Internet has limitations as a job search tool. Although many people have used it to get job leads, it has not worked well for far more. Too many assume they can simply add their resume to nationwide job banks, and employers will line up to hire them. Just as with the older approach of sending out lots of resumes, good things sometimes happen, but not often.

I recommend two points of view that apply to all job search methods, including the Internet:

> **Tip:** *If the Internet is new to you, I recommend a book titled Best Career and Education Web Sites, by Anne Wolfinger. It covers the basics plus lots of advice on using the Internet for career planning and job seeking.*

- It is unwise to rely on just one or two methods in conducting your job search.

- It is essential that you use an active rather than a passive approach in your job search.

Seven Ways to Increase the Effectiveness of Your Internet Job Search

I encourage you to use the Internet in your job search, but I suggest that you use it along with other techniques. Use the same sorts of job search techniques online as you do offline, including directly contacting employers and building up a network of personal contacts that can help you with your search. The following suggestions can increase the effectiveness of using the Internet in your job search.

Be as Specific as Possible in Identifying the Job You Seek

This is important in using any job search method, and it's even more important when you're looking for jobs on the Internet. The Internet is enormous, so it is essential to be as focused as possible in what you are searching for. Narrow your job title or titles to be as specific as possible. Limit your search to specific industries or areas of specialization. Locate and use specialized job banks in your area of interest.

Have Reasonable Expectations

Success on the Internet is more likely if you understand its limitations and strengths. For example, employers trying to find someone with skills in high demand, such as nurses, are more likely to use the Internet to recruit job candidates. Those who seek candidates in technical fields such as networking or database administration often use the Internet to find computer-savvy applicants.

Limit Your Geographic Options

If you don't want to move, or would move but only to certain areas, state this preference in your cover letter and restrict your search to those areas. Many Internet sites allow you to view or search for only those jobs that meet your location criteria.

Create an Electronic Resume

With few exceptions, resumes submitted on the Internet end up as simple text files with no graphic elements. Employers search databases of many resumes for those that include keywords or meet other searchable criteria. So create a simple text resume for Internet use and include words that are likely to be used by employers searching for someone with your abilities. (See Step 4 for more on creating an electronic resume.)

Get Your Resume into the Major Resume Databases

Most Internet employment sites let you add your resume for free, and then charge employers to advertise openings or to search for candidates. Although adding your resume to these databases is not enough in itself, doing so allows you to use your stored resume to easily apply for positions that are posted at these sites. These easy-to-use sites also often provide all sorts of useful information for job seekers.

Make Direct Contacts

Visit the Web sites of organizations that interest you and learn more about them. Many post openings, allow you to apply online, offer information on benefits and work environment, or even provide access to staff who can answer your questions. Even if they don't, you can always search the site or e-mail a request for the name of the person in charge of the work that interests you and then communicate with that person directly.

Network

You can network online, too, finding names and e-mail addresses of potential employer contacts or of other people who might know someone with job openings. Look at and participate in interest groups, professional association sites, alumni sites, chat rooms, e-mail discussion lists, and employer sites—these are just some of the many creative ways to network and interact with people via the Internet.

Useful Internet Sites

Thousands of Internet sites provide lists of job openings, information on careers or education, and related information. Many have links to other sites that they recommend. Service providers such as America Online (www.aol.com) and the Microsoft Network (www.msn.com) partner with sites such as Careerbuilder.com to include career information and job listings, plus links to other sites.

Here is a brief list of Web sites that are most used by job seekers, according to a recent survey, and ones that I recommend as being particularly useful. Although they are listed in categories, most list or link to sites with job openings, accept your resume, provide career and job search information, and provide links to related sites.

Web Sites with Good Links to Other Career Sites

- **Riley Guide** (www.rileyguide.com): Good information and lots of links to other career sites.

- **JIST** (www.jist.com): Free career information, links to other career sites, and resources.

Sites with Information on Careers and Industries

- **Career OINK** (www.CareerOINK.com): Provides descriptions for thousands of job titles and other good information, including the *OOH* job descriptions.

- **America's Career Information Network** (www.acinet.org): A federal government site with lots of industry and career information plus links to other sites.

Sites with Job Listings

General

- **America's Job Bank** (www.ajb.dni.us): Run by the U.S. Department of Labor.

- **Monster** (www.monster.com): The most-used site of all.

- **CareerBuilder** (careerbuilder.com).

- **Yahoo! HotJobs** (http://hotjobs.yahoo.com).

College Graduates

- **CollegeGrad.com** (www.collegegrad.com): Emphasis on entry-level jobs.

- **eRecruiting** (www.erecruiting.com): Jobs by region and specialty.

- **National Association of Colleges and Employers** (www.NACELink.com).

- **Job Central** (www.jobcentral.com): A joint site by NACE and employers.

Executive Jobs

- **6FigureJobs** (www.6figurejobs.com).

- **Career Journal** (www.CareerJournal.com): Affiliated with the *Wall Street Journal.*

- **Executives on the Web** (www.executivesontheweb.com).

Specialized Jobs

- **Dice** (www.Dice.com): Technology careers.

- **CareerBank** (www.CareerBank.com): Accounting and financial jobs.

- **Jobsinthemoney** (Jobsinthemoney.com): Accounting and financial jobs.

Diversity

- **LatPro** (www.latpro.com): For Latin American and bilingual professionals.

- **Hire Diversity** (www.hirediversity.com): Diversity recruiting and career development.

- **IMDiversity** (www.imdiversity.com): Job openings and advice for minorities and women.

International Jobs (English)

- **JobsDB** (www.jobsdb.com): Worldwide job openings.

- **Job Street** (www.jobstreet.com): Mostly Asian job opportunities.

- **Workopolis** (www.workopolis.com): Canadian job site.

Key Points: Step 3

- Use a variety of job search methods. The least effective include newspaper and Internet ads, filling out applications, employment agencies, and sending out lots of resumes or posting them on the Internet. Although these are all passive ways of looking for work, use them along with more effective methods because they do work for some people.

- The two most effective ways of finding job openings are developing a network of contacts and contacting employers directly. These are active job search methods.

- The Internet can be a helpful job search tool if you use it in active ways and combine it with other active methods.

Write a Simple Resume Now and a Better One Later

You've already learned that sending out paper resumes and waiting for responses is passive and not an effective job seeking technique. Posting your resume on one or more Internet sites is also passive, but is useful if used with more active approaches.

You can use your online resume to easily apply for jobs listed on online job banks, and have both an Internet and paper resume handy to use in your job search. The fact is that many employers *will* ask you for a paper or Internet resume, so a resume can be a useful tool in your job search. Unfortunately, too many people spend weeks working on their resume when they should be out getting interviews instead.

So I suggest that you begin with a simple resume you can complete quickly and start using today. If you want a "better" resume, you can work on improving it on weekends and evenings using the tips presented in this Step.

Tips for Creating a Superior Resume

The following are some basic tips that make sense for any resume format, paper or electronic.

Write It Yourself

It's okay to look at other resumes for ideas, but write yours yourself. It will force you to organize your thoughts and background, and you will be better able to discuss them in interviews.

Make It Error-Free

One spelling or grammar error will create a negative impressionist (see what I mean?). Get someone else to review your final draft for any errors. Then review it again because these rascals have a way of slipping in.

Make It Look Good

Poor copy quality, cheap paper, bad type quality, or anything else that creates a poor appearance will turn off employers to even the best resume content. Internet resumes have format rules of their own, and you will need to make them look presentable in that format. I give details on this later in this Step.

Get professional help with design and printing, if necessary. Many professional resume writers and even print shops offer writing and desktop design services.

Be Brief; Be Relevant

Many good resumes fit on one page, and few justify more than two. Include only the most important points. Use short sentences and action words. If it doesn't relate to and support the job objective, cut it!

Be Honest

Don't overstate your qualifications. If you end up getting a job you can't handle, who does it help? And a lie can result in you being fired later.

Be Positive

Emphasize your accomplishments and results. A resume is no place to be too humble or to display your faults.

Be Specific

Instead of saying "I am good with people," you can say, "I supervised four people in the warehouse and increased productivity by 30 percent." Use numbers whenever possible, such as the number of people served, the dollars saved, or the percentage by which sales increased.

> ### *Avoid the Resume Pile*
>
> Resume experts often suggest that a "dynamite" resume will jump out of the pile. This is old-fashioned advice. It assumes that you are applying to large organizations and for advertised jobs. Today, most jobs are with small employers and are not advertised. My advice is to avoid joining that stack of resumes in the first place by looking for openings that others overlook. See Step 3 for more on how to do this.

The Five Most Effective Ways to Use a Resume

Even an excellent resume won't get you talking with an employer unless you use it effectively. These tips suggest how to use your resume to get more interviews:

1. **Get the interview first.** It's always better to contact employers by phone, by e-mail, or in person before you send a resume. If possible, get a referral from someone you know. Or make a cold contact directly with the employer. In either case, ask for an interview. If no opening is available now, ask whether you can come in and discuss the possibility of future openings.

2. **Then send your resume.** Whenever possible, send or e-mail your resume after you schedule an interview, so that the employer can read about you before your meeting. You can then spend the valuable interview time discussing your skills rather than details that are best presented in a resume.

3. **Follow up with a JIST Card and thank-you note.** Immediately after an interview, send a thank-you note. Even if you use e-mail to communicate with employers, most appreciate a mailed thank-you note. And mailing the note enables you to enclose your JIST Card or another copy of your resume.

4. **Send your resume and JIST Card to everyone in your growing job search network.** This is an excellent way for people in your network to help you find unadvertised leads. They can pass or e-mail information to others who might be interested in a person with your skills.

5. **Send your resume in the traditional way only if you can't make direct contact.** In some situations, you can't easily make contact with an employer. This is true, for example, if you want to post your

resume on the Internet. Another example is when responding to a want ad that gives only a box number. Go ahead and do these things; just plan on using more active job search methods, too.

Types of Resumes

Generally the most common and useful resume types are the chronological resume, the skills (or functional) resume, and the combination resume. I also mention the curriculum vitae (CV), which is used for some specialized professional careers.

Chronological Resumes

The word "chronology" refers to a sequence of events in time. The primary feature of this type of resume is the listing of jobs you've held, arranged in reverse order from the most recent to least recent. This is the simplest of resumes and can be a practical format if you use it properly. I show you how to create this basic type of resume later in this Step.

Because a chronological resume organizes information by your work experience, it highlights previous job titles, locations, dates employed, and tasks. This is fine if you are looking for the same type of job you have held in the past or are looking to move up in a related field.

The chronological resume presents a career progression and allows employers to quickly screen out applicants whose backgrounds are not conventional or do not fit the preferred profile. The chronological format is often not good for people who have limited work experience (such as recent graduates), want to do something different, or have less-than-ideal work histories such as job gaps.

Skills, or Functional, Resumes

Rather than list your experience under each job, this resume style clusters your experiences under major skill areas. For example, if you are strong in "communication skills," you could list a variety of work and other experiences under that heading.

This format makes little sense, of course, unless your job objective *requires* these skills. For this reason and others, a skills resume is often more difficult to write than a simple chronological resume. But if you have limited paid work experience, are changing careers, or have not worked for a while, a skills resume might be a better way to present your strengths.

A skills resume is often used in situations where the writer wants to avoid displaying obvious weaknesses that would be highlighted on a chronological resume. For example, someone who has been a teacher but who now wants a career in sales could clearly benefit from a skills resume. A skills resume can help hide a variety of other weaknesses as well, such as limited work experience, gaps in job history, lack of educational credentials, and other flaws. This is one reason why some employers don't like skills resumes—they make it harder for them to quickly screen out applicants.

Personally, I like skills resumes. Assuming that you honestly present what you can do, a skills resume often gives you the best opportunity to present your strengths in their best light.

Combination and Other Creative Resumes

You can combine elements of both the chronological and skills formats in various ways to improve the clarity or presentation of a resume. This is often a good compromise when your experience is limited but an employer still wants to see a chronological listing of your work history (as many do). You can begin the resume with a skills format but still include a section that lists your jobs in order, along with the dates you held them.

There are also creative formats that defy any category but that are clever and have worked for some people. These resumes use innovative formats and styles. Some use dramatic graphics, colors, and shapes. I've seen hand-written resumes (usually *not* a good idea); unusual paper colors, sizes, and shapes; resumes with tasteful drawings and borders; and lots of other ideas. Some of these resumes were well done and well received; others were not. Graphic artists, for example, might use their resumes as examples of their work and include various graphic elements. An advertising or marketing person might use a writing style that approximates copy writing and a resume design that looks like a polished magazine ad.

The Curriculum Vitae and Other Special Formats

Attorneys, college professors, physicians, scientists, and various other occupations have their own rules or guidelines for preparing a "Professional Vitae" or some other special format. If you are looking for a job in one of these specialized areas, you should learn how to prepare a resume to those specifications. These specialized and occupation-specific resumes are not within the scope of this book and examples are not included, but many books provide information on these special formats, including *Expert Resumes for Teachers and Educators* by Wendy S. Enelow and Louise M. Kursmark.

Write a Chronological Resume

A chronological resume is easy to do. It works best for people who have had several years of experience in the same type of job they are seeking now. This is because a chronological resume clearly displays your recent work experience.

> **Tip:** *The important point is to get together an acceptable resume quickly so that you won't be sitting at home worrying about your resume instead of being out job hunting.*

Most employers will find a chronological resume perfectly acceptable, as long as it is neat and has no errors. You can use it early in your job search while you work on a more sophisticated resume.

Two Chronological Resume Samples

Two sample chronological resumes for the same person follow. The first (figure 4-1) is a simple one, but it works well enough in this situation because Judith is looking for a job in her present career field, has a good job history, and has related education and training. Note that she wants to move up in responsibility, and her resume emphasizes the skills and education that will assist her.

The second example (figure 4-2) is an improved version of this same resume. The improved resume adds a number of features, including a more thorough job objective, a Strengths and Skills section, and more accomplishments and skills. Notice, too, the impact of the numbers she adds to this resume in statements such as "top 30% of class" and "decreased department labor costs by more than $30,000 a year."

> **Tip:** *One nice feature is that Judith put her recent business schooling in both the Education and Experience sections. Doing this filled a job gap and allows her to present recent training as equivalent to work experience. This resume includes the extra Strengths and Skills section, where she presents some special strengths that often are not included in a resume.*

You should be able to do this sort of resume with an hour or two of additional work over the previous one. As I think you will realize, most employers will like the additional positive information it provides.

Figure 4-1: A simple chronological resume.

Judith J. Jones

115 South Hawthorne Avenue
Chicago, Illinois 66204
(312) 653-9217 (home)
email: jj@earthlink.net

JOB OBJECTIVE

Desire a position in the office management, accounting, or administrative assistant area. Prefer a position requiring responsibility and a variety of tasks.

EDUCATION AND TRAINING

Acme Business College, Lincoln, Illinois
Graduate of a one-year business program.

John Adams High School, South Bend, Indiana
Diploma, business education.

U.S. Army
Financial procedures, accounting functions.

Other: Continuing-education classes and workshops in business communication, computer spreadsheet and database programs, scheduling systems, and customer relations.

EXPERIENCE

2003–present—Claims Processor, Blue Spear Insurance Co., Willmette, Illinois. Handle customer medical claims, develop management reports based on spreadsheets I created, exceed productivity goals.

2002–2003—Returned to school to upgrade my business and computer skills. Took courses in advanced accounting, spreadsheet and database programs, office management, human relations, and new office techniques.

1999–2002—E4, U.S. Army. Assigned to various stations as a specialist in financial operations. Promoted prior to honorable discharge.

1998–1999—Sandy's Boutique, Wilmette, Illinois. Responsible for counter sales, display design, cash register, and other tasks.

1996–1998—Held part-time and summer jobs throughout high school.

PERSONAL

I am reliable, hardworking, and good with people.

Figure 4-2: An improved chronological resume.

Judith J. Jones

115 South Hawthorne Avenue
Chicago, Illinois 66204

jj@earthlink.net
(312) 653-9217

JOB OBJECTIVE

Seeking a position requiring excellent business management expertise in an office environment. Position should require a variety of skills, including office management, word processing, and spreadsheet and database application use.

EDUCATION AND TRAINING

Acme Business College, Lincoln, IL
Completed one-year program in Professional Office Management. Achieved GPA in top 30% of class. Courses included word processing, accounting theory and systems, advanced spreadsheet and database applications, graphics design, time management, and supervision.

John Adams High School, South Bend, IN
Graduated with emphasis on business courses. Earned excellent grades in all business topics and won top award for word-processing speed and accuracy.

Other: Continuing-education programs at own expense, including business communications, customer relations, computer applications, and sales techniques.

EXPERIENCE

2003–present—**Claims Processor, Blue Spear Insurance Company,** Wilmette, IL. Process 50 complex medical insurance claims per day, almost 20% above department average. Created a spreadsheet report process that decreased department labor costs by more than $30,000 a year. Received two merit raises for performance.

2002–2003—**Returned to business school to gain advanced office skills.**

1999–2002—**Finance Specialist (E4), U.S. Army.** Systematically processed more than 200 invoices per day from commercial vendors. Trained and supervised eight employees. Devised internal system allowing 15% increase in invoices processed with a decrease in personnel. Managed department with a budget equivalent of more than $350,000 a year. Honorable discharge.

1998–1999—**Sales Associate promoted to Assistant Manager, Sandy's Boutique,** Wilmette, IL. Made direct sales and supervised four employees. Managed daily cash balances and deposits, made purchasing and inventory decisions, and handled all management functions during owner's absence. Sales increased 26% and profits doubled during tenure.

1996–1998—**Held various part-time and summer jobs through high school while maintaining GPA 3.0/4.0.** Earned enough to pay all personal expenses, including car insurance. Learned to deal with customers, meet deadlines, work hard, and handle multiple priorities.

STRENGTHS AND SKILLS

Reliable, with strong work ethic. Excellent interpersonal, written, and oral communication and math skills. Accept supervision well, effectively supervise others, and work well as a team member. General ledger, accounts payable, and accounts receivable expertise. Proficient in Microsoft Word, Excel, and Outlook; WordPerfect.

Writing the Major Sections of a Chronological Resume

Now that you have seen what both basic and improved chronological resumes look like, it's time to do your own chronological resume. Use the Instant Resume Worksheet beginning on page 80 to complete each part of your basic chronological resume.

Name

This one seems obvious, but you want to avoid some things. For example, don't use a nickname—you need to present a professional image. Even if you have to modify your name a bit from the way you typically introduce yourself, it might be appropriate.

Mailing Address

Don't abbreviate words such as "Street" or "Avenue." Do include your ZIP code. If you might move during your job search, ask a relative, friend, or neighbor whether you can temporarily use his or her address for your mail. As a last resort, arrange for a post office box. Forwarded mail will be delayed and can cause you to lose an opportunity; get an address at the new location so that you appear to be settled there.

Phone Numbers and E-mail Address

An employer is more likely to phone or send an e-mail than to contact you by mail. So giving an employer this contact information is essential.

Let's start with the telephone. Use a phone number that will be answered throughout your job search. Always include your area code. Because you often will be gone (at your current job or out job seeking, right?), you must use an answering machine or voice mail. Phone companies sell voice-mail services for a monthly fee, including an option of a separate voice-mail phone number. This can pay off if you worry about how your calls might be answered at home. It takes only one messed-up message to make this service worthwhile.

> **Tip:** Keep in mind that an employer could call at any time. Make sure that anyone who will pick up the phone knows to answer professionally and take an accurate message, including a phone number. Practice with these people if you need to. Nothing is as maddening as a garbled message with the wrong number.

I suggest that you call your answering machine or voice-mail message. Listen to what it says, and how. If yours has some cute, boring, or less-than-professional message, change it to one you would like your next employer to hear. You can go back to your standard howling-wolves message after you get your next job.

As you look at this book's sample resumes, notice that some provide more than one phone number or an explanation following the number. For example, "555-299-3643 (messages)" quickly communicates that the caller is likely to leave a message rather than reach you in person. Adding "555-264-3720 (cell phone)" gives employers another calling option.

Be sure to include an e-mail address. Many employers prefer to e-mail candidates. You can get a free e-mail address from several places, including www.yahoo.com, www.hotmail.com, and www.google.com.

Now, take a moment to complete the Identification section in the Instant Resume Worksheet on page 80.

Job Objective

Although you could put together a simple resume without a job objective, it is wise to include one. Doing so will allow you to select resume content that will directly support the job you want.

Carefully write your job objective so that it does not exclude you from any jobs you would consider. For example, if you use a job title like "administrative assistant," ask yourself if doing so would exclude you from other jobs you would consider. Look at how Judith Jones presented her job objective in her basic resume (figure 4-1):

Desire a position in the office management, accounting, or administrative assistant area. Prefer a position requiring responsibility and a variety of tasks.

This objective opens up more options for her than if she simply said "administrative assistant." And her improved resume's job objective says even more:

Seeking position requiring excellent business management expertise in an office environment. Position should require a variety of tasks, including office management, word processing, and spreadsheet and database application use.

A good job objective allows you to be considered for more responsible jobs than you have held in the past or to accept jobs with different titles that use similar skills.

I see many objectives that emphasize what the person wants but that do not provide information on what he or she can do. For example, an objective that says "Interested in a position that allows me to be creative and that offers adequate pay and advancement opportunities" is not good. Who cares? This objective, a real one that someone wrote, displays a self-centered, "gimme" approach that will turn off most employers. Yours should emphasize what you can do, your skills, and where you want to use them.

Use the following worksheet to help you construct an effective and accurate Job Objective statement for your resume.

THE JOB OBJECTIVE WORKSHEET

1. **What sort of position, title, and area of specialization do you want?** Write the type of job you want, just as you might explain it to someone you know.

   _____

   _____

   _____

2. **Define your bracket of responsibility.** Describe the range of jobs you would accept, from the minimum up to those you think you could handle if you were given the chance.

   _____

   _____

   _____

(continued)

(continued)

3. **Name the key skills you have that are important in this job.** Describe the two or three key skills that are particularly important for success in the job that you are seeking. Select one or more of these that you are strong in and that you enjoy using. Write them here.

_____

_____

_____

4. **Name any specific areas of expertise or strong interest that you want to use in your next job.** If you have substantial interest, experience, or training in a specific area and want to include it in your job objective (remembering that it might limit your options), write it here.

_____

_____

_____

5. **What else is important to you?** Is there anything else you want to include in your job objective? This could be a value that is particularly important to you (such as "a position that allows me to help families" or "employment in an aggressive and results-oriented organization"), a preference for the size or type of organization ("a small- to mid-sized business"), or something else.

_____

_____

_____

Refer to the examples of simple but useful job objectives in the box on page 75. Most provide some information on the type of job the candidate seeks as well as on the skills he or she offers.

Sample Job Objectives

A responsible general-office position in a busy, medium-sized organization.

A management position in the warehousing industry. Position should require supervisory, problem-solving, and organizational skills.

Computer programming or systems analysis. Prefer an accounting-oriented emphasis and a solution-oriented organization.

Medical assistant or coordinator in a physician's office, hospital, or other health services environment.

Responsible position that requires skills in public relations, writing, and reporting.

An aggressive and success-oriented professional seeking a sales position offering both challenge and growth.

Desire position in the office-management area. Position should require flexibility, good organizational skills, and an ability to handle people.

The sample resumes in this Step include job objectives that you can review to see how others have phrased them. Browse these objectives for ideas.

Now jot down your own draft job objective and refine it until it "feels good." Then rewrite it on the Instant Resume Worksheet on page 80.

Tip: *The best objectives avoid a narrow job title and keep your options open to a wide variety of possibilities within a range of appropriate jobs.*

Education and Training

Lead with your strengths. Recent graduates or those with good credentials but weak work experience should put their education and training toward the top because it represents a more important part of their experience. More-experienced workers with work experience related to their job objective can put their education and training toward the end.

You can drop the Education and Training section if it doesn't support your job objective or if you don't have the credentials typically expected of those seeking similar positions.

Tip: *Drop or downplay details that don't support your job objective. For example, if you possess related education but not a degree, tell employers what you do have. Include details of related courses, good grades, related extracurricular activities, and accomplishments.*

This is particularly true if you have lots of work experience in your career area. Usually, though, you should emphasize the most recent or highest level of education or training that relates to the job.

Depending on your situation, your education and training could be the most important part of your resume, so beef it up with details if you need to.

On a separate piece of paper, rough out your Education and Training section. Then edit it to its final form and write it on pages 80–81 of the Instant Resume Worksheet.

Use Action Words and Phrases

Use active rather than passive words and phrases throughout your resume. Here is a short list of active words to give you some ideas:

Achieved	Established priorities	Organized
Administered	Expanded	Planned
Analyzed	Implemented	Presented
Controlled	Improved	Promoted
Coordinated	Increased productivity	Reduced
Created	(or profits)	expenses
Designed	Initiated	Researched
Developed	Innovated	Scheduled
Diagnosed	Instructed	Solved
Directed	Modified	Supervised
Established policy	Negotiated	Trained

Work and Volunteer History

This resume section provides the details of your work history, starting with the most recent job. If you have significant work history, list each job along with details of what you accomplished and special skills you used. Emphasize skills that directly relate to the job objective on your resume.

Treat volunteer or military experience the same way as other job experiences. This can be very important if this is where you got most of your work experience.

Previous Job Titles

You can modify the title you had to more accurately reflect your responsibilities. For example, if your title was sales clerk but you frequently opened and closed the store and were often left in charge, you might use the more descriptive title of night sales manager. Check with your previous supervisors if you are worried about this and ask whether they would object.

If you were promoted, you can handle the promotion as a separate job if it is to your advantage. Also make sure your resume mentions that you were promoted.

Previous Employers

Provide the organization's name and list the city, state, or province in which it was located. A street address or supervisor's name is not necessary—you can provide those details on a separate sheet of references if the employer asks for them.

Employment Dates

If you have large employment gaps that are not easily explained, use full years instead of months and years to avoid emphasizing the gaps. If there was a significant period when you did not work, did you do anything that could explain it in a positive way? School? Travel? Raise a family? Self-employment? Even if you mowed lawns and painted houses for money while you were unemployed, that could count as self-employment. It's much better than saying you were unemployed.

Duties and Accomplishments

In writing about your work experience, be sure to use action words and emphasize what you accomplished. Quantify what you did and provide evidence that you did it well. Take particular care to mention skills that directly relate to doing well in the job you want now.

If your previous jobs are not directly related to what you want to do now, emphasize skills you used in previous jobs that could be used in the new job. For example, someone who waits on tables has to deal with people and work quickly under pressure—skills that are needed in many other jobs such as accounting and managing.

Use separate sheets of paper to write rough drafts of what you will use in your resume. Edit it so that every word contributes something. When you're done, transfer your statements to pages 83–86 of the Instant Resume Worksheet.

Professional Organizations

This is an optional section where you can list job-related professional, humanitarian, or other groups with which you've been involved. These activities might be worth mentioning, particularly if you were an officer or were active in some other way. Mention accomplishments or awards. Many of the sample resumes in this Step include statements about accomplishments.

Now go to page 86 of the Instant Resume Worksheet and list your job-related efforts in professional organizations and other groups.

Recognition and Awards

If you have received any formal recognition or awards that support your job objective, consider mentioning them. You might create a separate section for them; or you can put them in the Work Experience, Skills, Education, or Personal sections.

Personal Information

Years ago, resumes included personal details such as height, weight, marital status, hobbies, leisure activities, and other trivia. Please do not do this. Current laws do not allow an employer to base hiring decisions on certain points, so providing this information can cause some employers to toss your resume. For the same reason, do not include a photo of yourself.

Although a Personal section is optional, I sometimes like to end a resume on a personal note. Some resumes provide a touch of humor or playfulness

Tip: Look up the descriptions of jobs you have held in the past and jobs you want now in the Occupational Outlook Handbook (see Step 3). You can also find free information on 14,000 different jobs at CareerOINK (www.careeroink.com). These descriptions will tell you the skills needed to succeed in the new job. Emphasize these and similar skills in your resume.

Tip: Emphasize accomplishments! Think about the things you accomplished in jobs, school, the military, and other settings. Make sure that you emphasize these things in your resume, even if it seems like bragging.

as well as selected positives from outside school and work lives. This section is also a good place to list significant community involvements, a willingness to relocate, or personal characteristics an employer might like. Keep it short.

Turn now to page 86 of the Instant Resume Worksheet and list any personal information you feel is appropriate.

References

It is not necessary to include the names of your references on a resume. You can do better things with the precious space. It's not even necessary to state "references available on request" at the bottom of your resume because that is obvious. If an employer wants your references, he or she knows to ask you for them.

It is helpful to line up references in advance. Pick people who know your work as an employee, volunteer, or student. Make sure they will express nice things about you by asking what they would say if asked. Push for negatives and don't feel hurt if you get some. Nobody is perfect, and it gives you a chance to delete references before they do you damage.

When you know who to include, create a clean list of references in a separate file. Include names, addresses, phone numbers, and details of why they are on your list. You can give this to employers who want it.

The Final Draft

At this point, you should have completed the Instant Resume Worksheet. Carefully review dates, addresses, phone numbers, spelling, and other details. You can now use the worksheet as a guide for preparing a better-than-average chronological resume.

Use the sample chronological resumes from this Step as the basis for creating your resume. Look them over for writing and formatting ideas.

Put the information from the worksheet into the form of a resume in a word-processing document. Most word-processing programs have resume templates or "wizards" that will

> **Tip:** Some employers have policies against giving references by e-mail or over the phone. If this is the case with a previous employer, ask the employer to write a letter of reference for you to photocopy as needed. This is a good idea in general, so you might want to ask employers for one even if they have no rules against phone references.

help make it look good. If you do not have access to a computer, have someone else do your resume. But whether you do it yourself or have it done, carefully review it for typographical or other errors that might have slipped in. Then, when you are certain that everything is correct, have the final version prepared.

INSTANT RESUME WORKSHEET

Identification

Name_____

Home address_____

ZIP code_____

Phone number and description (if any)_____

_____

Alternate phone number and description_____

_____

E-mail address_____

Your Job Objective

_____

_____

_____

_____

_____

_____

Education and Training

Highest Level/Most Recent Education or Training

Institution name_____

City, state/province (optional)_____

Certificate or degree_____

Specific courses or programs that relate to your job objective_____

_____

_____

Related awards, achievements, and extracurricular activities_____

_____

_____

Anything else that might support your job objective, such as good
grades_____

_____

_____

_____

_____

College/Post High School

Institution name_____

City, state/province (optional)_____

Certificate or degree_____

_____

Specific courses or programs that relate to your job objective_____

_____

_____

Related awards, achievements, and extracurricular activities_____

_____

_____

Anything else that might support your job objective, such as good
grades_____

_____

(continued)

(continued)

_____

_____

_____

High School

Institution name_____

City, state/province (optional)_____

Certificate or degree_____

Specific courses or programs that relate to your job objective_____

_____

_____

Related awards, achievements, and extracurricular activities_____

_____

_____

Anything else that might support your job objective, such as good grades_____

_____

_____

_____

_____

**Armed Services Training
and Other Training or Certification**

Institution name_____

Specific courses or programs that relate to your job objective_____

_____

_____

Related awards, achievements, and extracurricular activities_____

_____

_____

Anything else that might support your job objective, such as good grades_____

_____

_____

_____

_____

Related Workshops, Seminars, Informal Learning, or Any Other Training

_____

_____

_____

_____

_____

_____

Work Experience

Most Recent Position

Dates: from _____ to_____

Organization name_____

City, state/province_____

Your job title(s)_____

Duties_____

_____

_____

(continued)

(continued)

Skills _____

_____

_____

Equipment or software you used _____

_____

_____

Promotions, accomplishments, and anything positive _____

_____

_____

Next Most Recent Position

Dates: from _____ to _____

Organization name _____

City, state/province _____

Your job title(s) _____

Duties _____

_____

_____

Skills _____

_____

_____

Equipment or software you used _____

_____

_____

Promotions, accomplishments, and anything positive _____

_____

_____

Next Most Recent Position

Dates: from _____ to _____

Organization name_____

City, state/province_____

Your job title(s)_____

Duties_____

_____

_____

Skills_____

_____

_____

Equipment or software you used_____

_____

_____

Promotions, accomplishments, and anything positive_____

_____

_____

Next Most Recent Position

Dates: from _____ to _____

Organization name_____

City, state/province_____

_____

Your job title(s)_____

Duties_____

_____

_____

(continued)

(continued)

Skills_____

_____

_____

Equipment or software you used_____

_____

_____

Promotions, accomplishments, and anything positive_____

_____

_____

Any Other Work or Volunteer Experience

_____

_____

_____

_____

Professional Organizations

_____

_____

_____

_____

Personal Information

_____

_____

_____

_____

Writing Your Skills Resume

The skills resume format uses a number of sections similar to those in a chronological resume. Here I will discuss only those sections that are substantially different—the job objective and skills sections. The samples at the end of this Step give you ideas on skills resume language, organization, and layout, as well as how to handle special problems.

Don't be afraid to use a little creativity in writing your skills resume. Remember, you are allowed to break some rules if it makes sense.

Job Objective

Although a simple chronological resume does not require a career objective, a skills resume does. Without a reasonably clear job objective, you can't select and organize the key skills you have to support that job objective. The job objective statement on a skills resume should answer the following questions:

- **What sort of position, title, or area of specialization do you seek?** After reading the information on job objectives in the preceding section, you should know how to present the type of job you are seeking. Is your objective too narrow and specific? Is it so broad or vague that it's meaningless?

- **What level of responsibility interests you?** Job objectives often indicate a level of responsibility, particularly for supervisory or management roles. If in doubt, always try to keep open the possibility of getting a job with a higher level of responsibility (and, often, salary) than your previous or current one. Write your job objective to include this possibility.

- **What are your most important skills?** What are the two or three most important skills or personal characteristics needed to succeed on the job you're targeting? These are often mentioned in a job objective.

The Skills Section

This section can be called Areas of Accomplishment, Summary of Qualifications, Areas of Expertise and Ability, and so on. Whatever you choose to call it, this section is what makes a skills resume. To construct it, you must carefully consider which skills you want to emphasize.

Your task is to feature the skills that are essential to success on the job you want *and* that you have and want to use. You probably have a good idea of which skills meet both criteria.

Note that some resumes in this book emphasize skills that are not specific to a particular job. For example, "well organized" is an important skill in many jobs. In your resume, you should provide specific examples of situations or accomplishments that show you possess such skills. You can do this by including examples from previous work or other experiences.

The Key Skills List

Table 4.1 is a list of skills that are considered key for success on most jobs. It is based on research with employers about the skills they look for in employees. So if you have to emphasize some skills over others, include these—assuming you have them, of course.

Table 4.1: Key Skills Needed for Success in Most Jobs	
Basic Skills Considered the Minimum to Keep a Job	*Key Transferable Skills That Transfer from Job to Job and Are Most Likely Needed in Jobs with Higher Pay and Responsibility*
Basic academic skills	Instruct others
Accept supervision	Manage money and budgets
Follow instructions	Manage people
Get along well with co-workers	Meet the public
Meet deadlines	Work effectively as part of a team
Good attendance	Negotiating
Punctual	Organize/manage projects
Hard worker	Public speaking
Productive	Written and oral communication
Honest	Organizational effectiveness and leadership
	Self-motivation and goal setting
	Creative thinking and problem solving

In addition to the skills in the list, most jobs require skills specific to a particular job. For example, an accountant needs to know how to set up a general ledger, use accounting software, and develop income and expense reports. These job-specific skills are also called *job-content skills* and can be quite important in qualifying for a job.

IDENTIFY YOUR KEY TRANSFERABLE SKILLS

Look over the preceding key skills list and write down any skills you have that are particularly important for the job you want. Add other skills from page 11 of Step 2 that you feel must be communicated to an employer to get the job you want. Write at least three, but no more than five, of these most important skills:

1. _____

2. _____

3. _____

4. _____

5. _____

Prove Your Key Skills with a Story

Now, write each skill you listed in the preceding box on a separate sheet. For each skill, write several detailed examples of when you used it. If possible, you should use work situations, but you can use other situations such as volunteer work, school activities, or other life experiences. Try to quantify the examples by giving numbers such as money saved, sales increased, or other measures to support those skills. Emphasize results you achieved and any accomplishments.

The following is an example of what one person wrote for a key skill:

Key skill: Meeting deadlines

I volunteered to help my social organization raise money. I found out about special government funds, but the proposal deadline was only 24 hours away. So I stayed up all night and submitted it on time. We were one of only three groups whose proposals were approved, and we were awarded more than $100,000 to fund a youth program for a whole year.

Edit Your Key Skills Proofs

If you carefully consider the skills needed in the preceding story, there are quite a few. Here are some I came up with:

- Hard work

- Meeting deadlines

- Willing to help others

- Good written communication skills

- Persuasive

- Problem solver

Review each "proof sheet" and select the proofs that are particularly valuable in supporting your job objective. You should have at least two proof stories for each skill area. After you select your proofs, rewrite them using action words and short sentences. In the margins, write the skills you needed to do these things. When you're done, write statements you can use in your resume. Rewrite your proof statements and delete anything that does not reinforce the key skills you want to support.

Following is a rewrite of the sample proof story. Do a similar editing job on each of your own proofs until they are clear, short, and powerful. You can then use these statements in your resume, modifying them as needed.

Key skill: Meeting deadlines

On 24-hour notice, submitted a complex proposal that successfully obtained over $100,000 in funding.

You could easily use this same proof story to support other skills I listed earlier, such as hard work. So, as you write and revise your proof stories, consider which key skills they best support. Use the proofs to support those key skills in your resume.

Electronic and Scannable Resumes

A traditional resume is printed on paper. The Internet, many employers, and computerized resume banks now often require resumes to be in electronic form.

If you plan to use the Internet in your job search, you will need to submit your resume in electronic form. Once you do so on an online job bank, your resume is entered into a database that might be searched by many employers. You can also post your resume online as its own Web page. Employers can then find it by doing an Internet search for someone with your skills, and you can give the address out to employers when applying for jobs.

Even if you don't plan on actively using the Internet in your job search, you need to understand how electronic resumes work. Many employers are scanning the resumes they receive, or asking applicants to paste their electronic resumes into the online database when they apply.

Scanners are machines that convert your paper resume into electronic text. This allows employers to use a computer to quickly search hundreds or thousands of resumes to find qualified applicants. The computers look for keywords in the resumes—usually qualifications and skills that match the criteria needed for the open positions—and sort out the resumes with the most "hits."

Many larger employers use scanning technology. Your paper resume is likely to be scanned into a database without your knowing it.

Because electronic resumes are used differently than those on paper, it is important to understand how you can increase their effectiveness and their "readability" by a machine.

An Electronic Resume Should Have Lots of Keywords

Employers using electronic databases search for keywords in resumes. So, the more keywords you include, the more likely your resume will be selected. Keywords are words and phrases specific to the job you want. Here are some ways to find and present keywords on your resume:

- **Add a keyword section.** A simple technique is to add a section to your resume titled "Key Skills." You can then add keywords that aren't included elsewhere in your resume. When replying to particular job ads, you can also quickly add keywords that target the specific skills asked for in the ad, and then print a revised copy of your resume to turn in. (Be sure, though, that you actually have these skills!)

- **Include all your important skill words.** If you completed the worksheets in Steps 1 and 2, include the key skills documented there.

- **Think like a prospective employer.** List the jobs you want. Then think of the keywords employers are likely to use when searching a database.

- **Review job descriptions.** Carefully review descriptions for jobs you seek in major print references such as the *Occupational Outlook Handbook* and the *O*NET Dictionary of Occupational Titles.* Most large Web sites that list job openings have lots of employer job postings and job descriptions to review. Corporate Web sites often post information on job openings, another source of keywords. Make a list of keywords in descriptions of interest and include them in your resume. Because there are often two or three ways to describe the same specific skills, try to use both applicable keywords somewhere on your resume.

- **Be specific.** List certifications and licenses, name any software and machines you can operate, and include special language and abbreviations used in your field. Be comprehensive, too; instead of just saying "Microsoft Office," list the individual components ("Word, Excel, Access, PowerPoint") in case employers are searching for skill with one particular program.

For an Electronic Resume, a Simple Design Is Best

The databases that your resume goes into want only text, not design. Scanners introduce fewer errors when the text is simple. What this means is that your resume's carefully done format and design elements need to be taken out, and your resume must be reduced to the simplest text format. This also applies when you are pasting your resume into an online form for inclusion in a resume database. Follow these guidelines:

- No graphics
- No lines
- No bold, italic, or other text variations
- No bullets (use asterisks instead)

The sample resume section in figure 4-3 has been reformatted from a traditional "on-paper" format to one for e-mail submission or scanning. It has a plain look that is easily read by computers and keywords that increase its chances of being selected in a search.

Figure 4-3: A section from an electronic resume (from *Expert Resumes for Military-to-Civilian Transitions*, by Wendy S. Enelow and Louise M. Kursmark).

```
T. Richard Polawski
5252 Memory Lane, Shuffletown, NC 28217
704-365-1818 — trpolawski@carolina.rr.com

==========================================
CAREER GOAL

Position as Instructor in an environment focused on education, enlightenment, and
encouragement.

==========================================
KEY BENEFITS

* Exceptional ability to communicate technical information to end users. Have
provided end-user training and ongoing support in network, Internet/Web, and various
Microsoft applications (Windows, Outlook, Exchange).
* Offer a unique, valuable perspective gained from longevity in the field (11 years
with Microsoft Corporation), complemented by a passion for technology, an enjoyment
of training delivery, and an inner drive to remain on the cutting edge.
* Expertise in systematically troubleshooting network messaging problems, upgrading
hardware/software, and performing service work; received superlative grades in
courses in Pascal, Advanced Pascal, FORTRAN, COBOL, and C languages.

==========================================
INFORMATION TECHNOLOGY COMPETENCIES

* Microsoft Certified Systems Engineer (MCSE), 1997; Microsoft Certified
Professional (MCP), 1994: Design, install, maintain, troubleshoot, test, and repair
computer systems. Experienced in building and rebuilding computers and related
peripherals.
* Strong background in developing and evaluating new products and implementing
``best practices.'' Extensive experience in writing technical (including user-
training) procedures.

==========================================
RECENT EMPLOYMENT HISTORY

MICROSOFT CORPORATION, Charlotte, NC, 1993-Present
----------------------------
Product Support Engineer
----------------------------
Currently provide product support for MS Exchange: Troubleshoot message-flow
problems across various networks and the Internet, to include interfacing with Lotus
Domino and Novell GroupWise servers. Previously provided support for MS Word for
Windows and Macintosh. Wrote technical procedures for user functions, including
repair, optimization, and other customer requirements.
```

The key characteristics of this type of resume include

- Only one easy-to-scan font (sans-serif fonts such as Arial work best)
- No tab indentations (use the space bar to line up items)
- No line or paragraph indents
- No centering; align text to the left
- No tables (format your text manually)

Quick Tips to Reformat Your Paper Resume for an Electronic Database

Fortunately, you can easily take your existing resume and reformat it for electronic submission. Here are some quick tips for doing so:

1. Cut and paste your resume text into a new file in your word processor.

2. Eliminate any graphic elements, such as lines or images.

3. Set your margins so that text is no more than 65 characters wide. (Highlight a line and use the word count feature to check; select the "characters [with spaces]" option when counting.)

4. Use one easy-to-scan font, such as Courier, Arial, Helvetica, or Times New Roman. Eliminate bold, italic, and other font styles.

5. Introduce major sections with words in all uppercase letters, rather than in bold or a different font.

Effective Cover Letters

A cover letter is sent with and "covers" a resume. Different situations require different types of letters. As always, make certain that your correspondence makes a good impression.

You may find that you don't need to send many formal cover letters. Job seekers using the approaches I recommend get by with informal thank-you notes sent with resumes and JIST Cards. But certain types of jobs and some organizations require a more formal approach. Use your judgment.

Some Tips for Writing and Using Superior Cover Letters

Here are some suggestions to help you create and use cover letters that get the reader's attention and make them want to read your resume.

Target Your Letter

Typical reasons for sending a cover letter include responding to an ad, preparing an employer for an interview (the best reason!), and following up after a phone call or interview. Each of these letters needs a different approach.

Send It to Someone by Name

Get the name of the person who is most likely to supervise you. Call first to get an interview. Then send your letter and resume.

Get It Right

Make sure you get the person's name, organization name, and address right. Include the person's correct job title. Make sure that your letter does not contain grammatical and other errors; this creates a poor impression.

Be Clear About What You Want

If you want an interview, ask for it. If you are interested in the organization, say so. Give clear reasons why the company should consider you. If you're responding to an ad or following up on a phone call, be sure that your letter targets the specific skills the employer is asking for.

Be Friendly and Professional

A professional, informal style is usually best. Avoid a hard-sell, "Hire-me-now!" approach. No one likes to be pushed.

Make It Look Good

Just like a resume, correspondence to an employer must look good. Use good-quality paper and matching envelopes. A standard business format is good for most letters.

Follow Up

Remember that contacting an employer directly is much more effective than sending a letter. Don't expect letters to get you many interviews. They are best used to follow up after you have contacted the employer.

Sample Cover Letters

The following cover letters were written by Louise Kursmark and included in our book *15-Minute Cover Letter.* They apply to a variety of different situations.

Figure 4-4: Pre-interview, no specific job opening (Darryl Poston).

Comments: This letter illustrates how the writer has built upon a casual in-person meeting to initiate a formal discussion about future career options. Although no job opening exists, he is wise in assuming that there will be one in the future. He is planting the seeds to be first in line when an opening does occur. Not only that, he is strengthening his professional network and making himself more visible and memorable within the new industry he is trying to penetrate.

DARRYL T. POSTON

4525 Carmel Court, Indianapolis, IN 46210
317-204-8040 ▪ darrylposton@aol.com

April 30, 2005

Sharon Hanrahan, Sales Manager
Alpha Omega Services
252 Court Street
Indianapolis, IN 46201

Dear Sharon:

I am looking forward to meeting with you on Friday to continue the conversation we started at last month's Downtowners event. We agreed that one of the characteristics of a successful sales professional is persistence. Now that I've more thoroughly researched your company, I don't intend to give up trying until I am successful in joining one of the best sales teams in the business and one of the best organizations in town!

My sales background is strong. In each of the last four years, in two different sales positions, I have exceeded my sales goals by 10% or more. I attribute this success to superior closing skills and dedication to every step of the sales process.

Since January, my performance has been measured by how well I continue selling after the initial sale is made. Customers come to me after they have decided to purchase a new car, and I sell them financing plans and add-on features and services. By carefully listening to my customers' needs and recommending the add-ons that are right for them, I have sold more extended service plans and dealer-installed stereo systems than anyone in my position in the last five years.

I'm confident I can deliver similar results for Alpha Omega, and I am eager to be part of your team.

If you have any questions before our meeting, please contact me by phone or email. Otherwise, I look forward to seeing you at 3 pm on Friday.

Sincerely,

Darryl T. Poston

attachment

Figure 4-5: No interview is scheduled (Brett Samuelson).

Comments: This letter makes an immediate connection with the recipient by mentioning a referral from a professional association. This type of connection can be an excellent source of contacts and job leads. Note that the writer will call again to arrange an appointment. This is an effective message because it leaves the ball firmly in the job seeker's court. Instead of relying on a busy executive to pick up the phone, the person with the most at stake (you, the job seeker) should persist in seeking a telephone conversation and ultimately an in-person meeting.

BRETT SAMUELSON

295 Skyline Drive, Ft. Thomas, KY 41015
Home 859-349-9076 • Mobile 859-208-0987 • brett@samuelson.com

April 30, 2005

Mr. Thomas Elder
Director of Marketing
Sabatino Specialties, Inc.
259 Vine Street
Cincinnati, OH 45202

Dear Mr. Elder:

Rachel Koehler (current president of the Cincinnati Chapter of the American Marketing Association) suggested that I contact you about marketing opportunities that you may know of in your role as chairman of the Cincinnati Incubator marketing board. I hope you received my voice-mail message on Monday—as promised, I am following up with more information.

I recently married and relocated to the Cincinnati area, and I am eager to find a young technology company that needs an experienced marketing professional to help introduce its innovations to various business markets.

My background and interests are a good fit for emerging high-tech companies. Since completing my MBA, I've helped two fledgling software developers gain solid traction in their markets. I understand how to position and present new technology concepts to business audiences (emphasizing business benefits, not just technology advances).

I will call you early next week to follow up. I appreciate any ideas, referrals, or assistance you can offer!

Sincerely,

Brett Samuelson

P.S.   The enclosed resume provides more detailed information about my experience, expertise, and track record.

Figure 4-6: Unsolicited resume sent to obtain an interview (Jennifer Tolles).

Comments: In this letter, the candidate makes an immediate connection by referring to a recent news article that featured the school system to which she is applying. Her bullet points make additional connections to what she learned about the school district. This helps send the message that she understands and fits into the unique culture of that organization. Notice how she indicates that she will call in hopes of setting up a meeting. Although she could not make a connection beforehand, she will work diligently to establish one after the fact.

Jennifer Tolles

75 Bolivar Terrace, Reading, MA 01867
jennifertee@aol.com
781-592-3409

April 30, 2005

Dr. Mark B. Cronin, Superintendent
Belmont Public Schools
644 Pleasant Street
Belmont, MA 02478

Dear Dr. Cronin:

Your school district's reputation for *excellence in education*—described so vividly in the recent *New England Journal of Elementary Education*—has prompted me to forward my resume for consideration for fall teaching positions. In addition to strong professional qualifications, you will find that I also have the intangible personal qualities that fit your culture and enable me to truly make a difference to the children I teach.

Please consider my qualifications:

- Recent bachelor's degree and Massachusetts teaching certification, grades 1–8.

- Year-long teaching experience as an LD Tutor for elementary and high school students—experience adapting classroom materials for individual students, delivering individual and group lessons, working collaboratively with classroom teachers, and promoting a positive learning environment for my students.

- Diverse field-teaching experiences (grades 1, 4, and 6); successful experience planning and delivering integrated lessons that sparked students' interest, creativity, and desire to learn.

- Keen respect for each individual child and appreciation for the differences among us.

- A highly effective classroom-management style that creates an environment in which all children can learn.

I will call you within a few days to see when it might be convenient to meet. Thank you for your consideration.

Sincerely,

Jennifer Tolles

enclosure

Four bulleted statements highlight this individual's most-important qualifications.

John Carpenter

40 Watertown Street
Binghamton, New York 13747

(607) 666-9999
hammertime@aol.com

Chief Estimator/Project Manager

Qualifications

- **Five years of experience as Chief Estimator and Project Manager.**
- **Fifteen-plus years of local engineering, design and construction expertise** in the upstate New York building industry, preparing bid estimates and managing $300,000 to $3 million construction projects.
- **Senior construction generalist with a diverse skills.** Excel within small construction companies that require "wearing many hats." Proven expertise in business development; project management for both fieldwork and administrative projects; estimating via computer applications; drafting and architectural drawing; and management of shop, carpentry and millworking operations.
- **Innovative information manager.** Repeatedly automated bidding and construction processes for past employers, increasing production and decreasing overhead. Advanced user:

  AutoCAD version 10, Generic CAD version 6, Construction Management Systems estimating software, Super Project, Varco Pruden, VP Command building design and drafting program, Novell Networking, Access, Excel, Lotus 1-2-3, Microsoft Office, GTCO digitizer tablets and HP Draft Pro Plotter.

Education and Credentials

A.A.S. Degree, Construction Technology: State University of New York, Canton College, 1984
Certified Engineer Technician: A.S.C.E.T. Professional Engineering Society.

Estimating Experience

Estimator and Project Manager   1999 — present
JAMES SMITH AND SONS CONTRACTING COMPANY, Vestal, New York
Utilize in-depth knowledge of project costs, purchasing, construction techniques and technology, and local construction services market to estimate and manage large construction projects.

- Bid and supported 4 major contract wins in FY2001, cumulatively valued at $6 million.
- Manage estimating projects that generated over $10,000 per month in gross sales FY2001.
- As chief estimator, identify upcoming opportunities and generate 3–4 project estimates a month.
- Win 1 of every 3 estimates the company decides to submit.
- Manage a millwork shop generating $400,000 in annual gross sales with 30% net profits.

Accomplishment statements are brief yet powerful.

Chief Estimator and Project Manager   1994 — 1999
ARCHER AND SONS, Binghamton, New York
Prepared estimates, assisted proposal and business development team, and managed major construction projects throughout New York State.

- Projects included: The Marriott Hotel, Cornell University; The Law School Renovation Project, Cornell University; various Taco Time Restaurants; and school building upgrades in upstate New York.
- All projects came in on time, within 10% of originally prepared cost estimates.

Estimator/AutoCAD Drafter
WAY-LAN CONSTRUCTION COMPANY, INC., Binghamton, New York   1985 — 1993

Figure 4-10: Submitted by Alice Hanson.

This one page resume uses several techniques to present his experience effectively in few words. The informal type font helps separate it from the "usual."

JOHN DOE

823 7th Avenue, Nicetown, Minnesota 55555 ● 555-555-5555

MACHINIST
Specialization in Wire Electrical Discharge Machining

One and one half years experience working in Wire EDM using Mitsubishi machines and programming Espirit CNCs. Certified in Safety and Wild Fire Training. Two years high school Spanish.

Lists key adaptive and transferable skills

Hard working, reliable team player with favorable attendance record. Able to work under pressure and with tight deadlines. Effective at prioritizing and decision making regarding part schedules and due dates. Strong sense of responsibility and maturity. Easily able to adapt to changing work environment or industry trends.

Friendly and easy to get along with. Sense of humor and positive communication skills.

EDUCATION

Rochester Community and Technical College, Minnesota
- Diploma in Machine Tool Technology, 19XX
- Other courses: math, psychology, sociology, health

TECHNICAL AND TECHNOLOGY SKILLS

A very efficient way to present job-related skills →

- Read Blueprints and Schematics
- CAD
- Electrical Discharge Machines
- CNC Milling Machine
- Wire EDM
- Drip Torches
- PC with Windows 95/98
- Internet and Search Engines
- Netscape

- Lathes
- Grinders and Sanders
- Sheet Metal Cutters
- Sheet Metal Brakes
- Paint Spray Guns
- Sand Blasters
- Chain Saws
- ATVs
- Forklifts

WORK HISTORY

Less detail needed here, since it is included elsewhere

HEAD MACHINIST, Smith's Shop, Nicetown MN
Load programs and perform machine setups. Run and inspect parts, comparing to blueprints. Operate CAD programs. 19XX TO present

MECHANIC'S HELPER, City of Rochester, MN   Summers 19XX, 19XX, 19XX

WORKER FOR MINNESOTA DEPARTMENT OF CONSERVATION CORP.
Department of Natural Resources   19XX

Figure 4-11: Submitted by Beverley Drake.

Functional headings identify both specific skills and personal attributes that have led to significant success for this young accountant.

Jonathan Radeux

radeux@hotmail.com
1590 134th Avenue S.E. Apt 107
Vancouver, WA 99800

(425) 555-2222

ACCOUNTANT / TAX

Relationship Manager — Self motivated and resourceful, demonstrating effective communication skills, sound judgment, and ability to complete tasks in a highly professional manner.

Team Player — Repeatedly commended for "going the extra mile" to deliver superior results.

Knowledgeable — Internal & External Audits ● Internal Revenue Code ● R&D Studies ● FAS 109 ● Tax Research ● Tax Projections ● Deferred Taxes ● SEC Reporting

EDUCATION

CPA — CPA Candidate ● Test scheduled May 2002.

Formal — University of Washington, Seattle, WA
Master of Professional Accounting, 2000 ● Concentration: Tax ● GPA 3.4
B.A. Business Administration, 1999 ● Concentration: Accounting ● GPA 3.2

Professional — PricewaterhouseCoopers, LLP
Tax Consulting Foundation Training, 2000 ● 50 hours
Tax Update, 2001

Computers — Proficient in the use of Microsoft Office (Windows, Excel, PowerPoint, Word, Access) ● LexisNexis ● Westlaw ● CCH & RIA databases ● Oracle Financial ● Lotus Notes ● Microsoft Exchange ● Visio ● Windows NT

PROFESSIONAL EXPERIENCE

Staff Associate, Tax & Legal Services Group — PRICEWATERHOUSECOOPERS, LLP, Portland, OR ● 2000–2001

Surpassed normal reporting hierarchy, directly supporting Senior Manager and Partner on M&A and FAS 109 analysis, deferred tax studies, and R&D tax credit projects for major companies.

Worked at client sites 80% of time, interviewing and interfacing with a wide range of professionals: lawyers, senior technology engineers, tax directors, tax managers, vice presidents, and technology product managers.

Accomplishment statements detail this person's success.

- Established 80% utilization rate, 30% over average for local tax associates, by aggressively seeking new challenges and projects.
- Only Staff Associate in Portland tax office to earn performance bonus in 2000.
- Assigned increasingly challenging projects based on performance, initiative, teamwork, and professionalism.

Intern, Tax Compliance — ROTHCHILD WENSON & COMPANY, PLLC, Vancouver, WA ● 1999
Federal and State Compliance. 1120S, 1065, 1040, and 1041 forms.

AFFILIATIONS

Oregon Society of Certified Public Accountants
Bonded, Oregon and Washington States
Notary, Oregon and Washington States

Figure 4-12: Submitted by Alice Hanson.

Note the many acronyms and banking terms in this resume. These are used to paint this person as an insider and as an expert in his field.

JAMES ROBERTS

10 Lake Street, Ramsey, New Jersey 07640
Pager: (212) 654-3278 ■ Home: (212) 324-9834 ■ E-mail: Jroberts@aol.com

RETAIL LOAN OFFICER

Proactive, results-oriented mortgage specialist with extensive experience in originating, processing and closing mortgage loans. Skilled in analyzing client needs and recommending appropriate mortgage products. Expertise with following types of loans: Conventional, ARMS, Jumbo, FHA, COFI, IndyMac, HELs, and HELOCs.

SUMMARY OF QUALIFICATIONS

- Over 6 years' experience in originating and closing mortgage loans.
- Outstanding record in converting referrals to closed loans. Effective in overcoming rate objections.
- Excellent interpersonal and communication skills; sensitive to customer needs.
- Honest, energetic, hardworking, and analytical; excellent decision-making capabilities.

RELEVANT EXPERIENCE & ACCOMPLISHMENTS

2000–Present **FINANCIAL SERVICES CONSULTANT**
ERA FINANCIAL SERVICES, Demarest, New Jersey
Wholly owned subsidiary of ERA Realtors. Report to Regional VP of Sales. Submit complete and accurate mortgage applications for underwriting. Cross-sell insurance and title services. *) job duties*

- Successfully closed over $15.2 million in loans in 10 months.
- Manage on average 20 loans with a $6 million pipeline.
- Developed close and loyal relationships with many in-house realtors.
- Achieved Ambassador Club designation for exceeding income goals.

Accomplishments (set apart with bullets) are clearly distinguished from job-duties and contain lots of solid numbers that add credibility.

1997–2000 **MORTGAGE LOAN OFFICER**
NORTHWEST MORTGAGE CORPORATION, Totowa, New Jersey
Large New Jersey mortgage company. Submitted mortgage applications for underwriting. Handled mortgage needs of 4 bank branches. Involved in marketing and promotion of mortgage services. Received extensive sales training.

- Recipient of "Gold Circle" award for 1998 and 1999 for being a top 10% producer.
- Tripled income within 3 years.
- Initiated and closed $43 million in loans. Managed on average 30 loans with an $8 million pipeline.
- Maintained 94% customer satisfaction rating while exceeding profitability requirements.

1995–1997 **MORTGAGE LOAN OFFICER**
SMITH & KOLINSKY, New York, New York
Regional mortgage broker specializing in co-ops and condominiums in New York City. Initiated and processed mortgage loans. Selected banks for loan approvals. Developed key banking relationships.

- Expanded business by networking with various contacts and building relationships with New Jersey banks.

1986–1995 **SENIOR CORPORATE FOREIGN EXCHANGE ADVISOR**
HONG KONG AND SHANGHAI BANKING CORPORATION, New York, New York
Large, full-service bank. Bought and sold foreign exchange, executed customer orders as required, and developed relationships with banks and analysts. Trained and managed new traders.

- Grew business by significantly increasing number of Fortune 500 customers.
- Promoted twice for superior performance.

EDUCATION

MBA–Finance, Fordham University, New York, New York 1986
BBA–Finance, Magna Cum Laude, Manhattan College, New York, New York 1981

Figure 4-13: Submitted by Igor Shpudejko.

Carla Rossini

55555 Bedford Drive
Camarillo, California 93010
Tel: (805) 555-1111
E-Mail: chefxtrodnry@yahoo.com

cooking philosophy
("rossini's rules" — posted in my kitchens)

- *Good Food is Art and We Are the Artists*
- *Good Food is Second Only to Customer Satisfaction*
- *Everybody is Somebody in My Kitchen*

professional profile

CERTIFIED EXECUTIVE CHEF — American Culinary Federation (ACF)
- Over 10 years' food preparation and kitchen management experience ranging from high-volume buffet (2000+ meals per day), to hotel, to intimate bistro settings
- California School of Culinary Arts "Le Cordon Bleu" graduate
- Continuing education in contemporary cuisine through Culinary Institute of America (CIA)
- Management expertise includes cost- and quality-control metrics, food-service management, dining-room service and supervision, beverage management, and management information systems (MIS/PC)
- Culinary proficiency in tableside cooking, baking / pastry / patisserie, charcuterie, cold buffet preparation, nutritional / dietary cooking, menu development, global cuisine (Classical, Nouvelle, American, Pacific Rim, Middle East, Latin), presentation, and environmental design
- Multilingual (English, Spanish, Italian) — Team Builder — Thrive in a high-energy environment

influences

- Mary Sue Milliken/Susan Feniger *(for their passionate seasonings)*
- Iron Chef Masaharu Morimoto *(for his food artistry and spontaneity)*
- Wolfgang Puck *(for his marketing genius and interior design)*
- Julia Child *(who brought classical cuisine into all our homes via TV)*

professional experience

EXECUTIVE CHEF (1998–PRESENT), L'AUGBERGINE RESTAURANT, CAMARILLO, CA
[Provençal and Mediterranean cuisine with a French country inn theme]
Collaborate with owner, sommelier, pastry and sous chefs on introduction of one new item weekly. Monitor market/vendor prices for ticket adjustment. Implement customer-driven improvements within cost constraints.
- Created a steady "happy hour" following by writing a press release describing our cold table (tapas, antjitos, hors-d'oeuvres) as "fast food for the seasoned palate."
- Planted a vegetable garden to ensure a ready supply of the freshest herbs and seasonal vegetables. The garden also increased the ambiance of the patio dining area.
- Added 4 outdoor natural gas heaters: Installation costs were recouped within 2 months of installation. Clientele doubled during traditionally slower winter months.

recent inventions

- *Tartare of belly tuna with Thai chili-infused pine nut oil*
- *Curaçao-lime sorbet*

ROOM SERVICE CHEF (HEAD) & KITCHEN MANAGER (1996–1998), RADISSON RESORT HOTEL, OXNARD, CA *[1,000+ room hotel and spa]*
Demonstrated versatility in delivering on-demand, 24/7, VIP and unusual orders from ingredients on hand. Streamlined kitchen procedures and supply usage in terms of product quality, efficiency, and economy. Directed and trained 20–30 food service employees in food preparation, presentation, and sanitation.
- Implemented an Excel first in/first out (FIFO) system to insure ingredient freshness.
- Introduced a Pacific Rim menu that resulted in 25% jump in patronage by Asian customers.
- Promoted to Head Room Service Chef & Kitchen Manager from Assistant in 1996.

FOOD SERVICE MANAGER (1990–1995), FURR'S CAFETERIA, OXNARD, CALIFORNIA
Supervisor for over 50 employees in a public cafeteria/buffet serving up to 2000 diners daily. Oversaw and trained food-service workers in food preparation, area sanitation, and personal hygiene. Scheduled work shifts. Assessed employee performance and resolved work-related problems. Controlled expenditures (e.g., food, supplies, utilities, and salaries) for conformance with corporate financial parameters. Ensured all activities reflected well on the company standards.
- Raised establishment's County sanitation rating from B to A within first 3 months on board.
- Instituted a local employee incentive award in the form of a paid day off for the employee of the quarter.

professional training

CALIFORNIA SCHOOL OF CULINARY ARTS, PASADENA, CA (1995–1996)
- Le Cordon Bleu Culinary Arts Program — Graduate

THE CULINARY INSTITUTE OF AMERICA (CIA) AT GREYSTONE, ST. HELENA, CA
- Continuing Education toward the American Culinary Federation (ACF) Master Chef Certificate expected 2003

The creative format of this resume met the challenge of showcasing this chef's superb education, creativity, and accomplishments.

Figure 4-14: Submitted by Roleta Fowler Vasquez.

A recommendation from a credible source — a school principal — leads off this functional-style resume.

EILEEN M. McFADDEN

(973) 548-9002 — PO Box 203, Morristown, NJ 07960 — eileenmac@hotmail.com

*E*ileen is an outstanding teacher who spends long hours preparing lessons and activities that foster individual talents and capabilities of her students — a seemingly overwhelming task with 35 children! I am constantly amazed at the progress of her children and their enthusiasm for learning. They love their teacher and really do their best in such a positive, nurturing atmosphere. — Principal, Moreford School

Experienced Elementary Educator
Early Childhood Specialist

Resourceful, caring teacher accomplished in assessing young children's abilities and needs to enhance literacy development and early language acquisition. Outstanding class management skills promote an inviting learning environment while maintaining discipline in the classroom.

Contributions

Her teaching experience is listed below without detail, while her contributions are grouped front-and-center for greatest impact.

✓ Conceive, produce and direct annual "Kindergarten Graduation" performance program. Received numerous kudos over the past 8 years from parents and faculty for perennially successful ceremony.

✓ Introduced Kindergarten Screening Program based on Brigance Program to identify and recommend appropriate placement of special needs and at-risk students.

✓ Create "Kindergarten Books" and "Reading Books" for each student to document progress throughout the year and apprise parents of continually evolving skills.

✓ Promote positive teacher-student-parent alliances by volunteering to assist with numerous extracurricular activities such as Drama Club, Latchkey Program and Field Day Games.

Education

Master of Science in Education and Bachelor of Arts in Psychology
William Paterson College, Paterson, NJ

Credentials

New Jersey State Certification — Elementary and Nursery
New York State Permanent Certification — N–6
New York City Teaching License

Selected In-Service Workshops

Attention Deficit Disorder, Emergent Literacy (2 years), Reporting Child Abuse, Reading Workshop (2 years), Agriculture in the Classroom
Milltown High School, Milltown, NJ (1991–Present)

Math/Science Workshop (3 years), Computers in the Classroom, Math/Computer Workshop
Morris County Community College, Morristown, NJ (Summers 1991–1997)

Teaching Experience

Moreford School, Milford, NY (1987–Present)
Kindergarten, 1991–Present… **Grade 1,** 1989–1991… **Pre-K,** 1987–1989

Frances Smith Elementary School, New York, NY (1980–1987)
Kindergarten and Grade 1

Figure 4-15: Submitted by Meg Guiseppi.

Key Points: Step 4

- To create a superior resume, keep these tips in mind: write it yourself, make it error-free, make it look good, keep it brief and relevant, be honest, be positive, and be specific.

- The five most effective ways to use a resume include getting the interview first before sending the resume, following up from the interview with a resume and JIST Card, sending your resume to people in your network, and sending your resume in the traditional way only if you can't make direct contact first.

- The three most common types of resumes are the chronological, the functional/skills, and the creative/combination. CVs are used primarily in the education and medical fields.

- Electronic resumes should contain lots of keywords and have a very simple format that can be read by scanners and computer databases.

- Effective cover letters are targeted to a particular person, error-free, clear, friendly, professional, and attractive.

Redefine What Counts as an Interview, and Then Organize Your Time to Get Two a Day

The average job seeker gets about five interviews a month—fewer than two a week. Yet many job seekers use the methods in this book to get two interviews a day. Getting two interviews a day equals 10 a week and 40 a month. That's 800 percent more interviews than the average job seeker gets.

Who do you think will get a job offer quicker?

However, getting two interviews a day is nearly impossible unless you redefine what counts as an interview. If you consider an interview in a different way, getting two a day is quite possible.

The New Definition of an Interview

An interview is any face-to-face contact with someone who has the authority to hire or supervise a person with your skills—even if no opening exists at the time you talk to them.

If you use this new definition, it becomes *much* easier to get interviews. You can now interview with all sorts of potential employers, not just those who have job openings now. While most other job seekers look for advertised or actual openings, you can get interviews before a job opens up or before it is advertised and widely known. You will be considered for jobs that may soon be created but that others will not know about. And, of course, you can also interview for existing openings as everyone else does.

Spending as much time as possible on your job search and setting a job search schedule are important parts of Step 5. If you are a student or are working now, set aside what time you can for job seeking. Later, when you can look full time, plan in advance to spend full time looking for your next job.

Make Your Search a Full-Time Job

Job seekers average fewer than 15 hours a week looking for work. On average, unemployment lasts three or more months, with some people out of work far longer (for example, older workers and higher earners). My many years of experience researching job seekers indicates that the more time you spend on your job search each week, the less time you will likely remain unemployed.

Of course, using the more effective job search methods presented in this book also helps. Many job search programs that teach job seekers my basic approach of using more effective methods and spending more time looking have proven that these seekers often find a job in half the average time. More importantly, many job seekers also find better jobs using these methods.

So, if you are unemployed and looking for a full-time job, you should plan to look on a full-time basis. It just makes sense to do so, although many do not, or they start out well but quickly get discouraged. Most job seekers simply don't have a structured plan—they have no idea what they are going to do next Thursday. The plan that follows will show you how to structure your job search like a job.

Decide How Much Time You Will Spend Looking for Work Each Week and Day

First and most importantly, decide how many hours you are willing to spend each week on your job search. You should spend a minimum of 25 hours a week on hard-core job search activities with no goofing around. The following worksheet walks you through a simple but effective process to set a week's job search schedule.

PLAN YOUR JOB SEARCH WEEK

1. How many hours are you willing to spend each week looking for a job?_____

2. Which days of the week will you spend looking for a job?

   _____

   _____

   _____

3. How many hours will you look each day?_____

   _____

   _____

4. At what times will you begin and end your job search on each of these days?_____

   _____

   _____

   _____

   _____

   _____

   _____

   _____

Create a Specific Daily Job Search Schedule

Having a specific daily schedule is essential because most job seekers find it hard to stay productive each day. The sample daily schedule that follows is the result of years of research into what schedule gets the best results. I tested many schedules in job search programs I ran, and this particular schedule worked best.

Consider using a schedule like this, or review the sample daily schedule for ideas on creating your own.

Time Is Money

The daily schedule you see on this page is based on my years of managing results-oriented job search programs. As simple as it seems, keeping a schedule like this will cut your job search time. Many thousands have used it as a basis for their daily job search plan, and it does work.

A Sample Daily Schedule That Works	
Time	*Activity*
7 a.m.	Get up, shower, dress, eat breakfast.
8–8:15 a.m.	Organize work space, review schedule for today's interviews and promised follow-ups, update schedule as needed.
8:15–9 a.m.	Review old leads for follow-up needed today; develop new leads from want ads, yellow pages, the Internet, warm contact lists, and other sources; complete daily contact list.
9–10 a.m.	Make phone calls and set up interviews.
10–10:15 a.m.	Take a break.
10:15–11 a.m.	Make more phone calls, set up more interviews.
11 a.m.–Noon	Send follow-up notes and do other "office" activities as needed.
Noon–1 p.m.	Lunch break, relax.
1–3 p.m.	Go on interviews, make cold contacts in the field.
Evening	Read job search books, make calls to warm contacts not reachable during the day, work on a "better" resume, spend time with friends and family, exercise, relax.

If you are not accustomed to using a daily schedule book or electronic planner, promise yourself to get a good one tomorrow. Choose one that allows plenty of space for each day's plan on an hourly basis, plus room for daily to-do lists. Write in your daily schedule in advance, and then add interviews as they come. Get used to carrying it with you—and use it!

A variety of computer programs can be used to help organize your job search. And pocket-sized electronic schedulers can be very helpful. If you have these resources, adapt the advice I have provided in this step to use these tools. If you don't use electronic tools, a simple schedule book and other paper systems will work just fine.

Key Points: Step 5

- Redefine what counts as an interview to include any face-to-face contact with someone who has the authority to hire or supervise a person with your skills—even if no opening exists at the time you talk to them.

- If you are unemployed, you should spend at least 25 hours a week on your job search and make it your full-time job.

- Creating a specific job search schedule and sticking to it will help you be more productive and find a job faster.

Step 6

Dramatically Improve Your Interviewing Skills

The interview is the most important 60 minutes in the job search. A great deal is at stake, yet the research indicates that most people are not well-prepared for the interview process. This lack of preparation can be good news for you, because reading this book can help you substantially improve your interviewing skills, thereby giving you an advantage over the majority of job seekers.

I have observed many employers who are willing to hire people who present themselves well in an interview over others with superior credentials. This chapter is based on substantial research into how employers decide on hiring one person over another. Although the interview itself is an incredibly complex interaction, I have found that there are simple things you can do that make a big difference in getting a job offer. This chapter presents some of the things I have learned over the years, and I hope you find them helpful.

Your First Impression May Be the Only One You Make!

Some research suggests that if the interviewer forms a negative impression in the first five minutes of an interview, your chances of getting a job offer approach zero. I know from experience that many job seekers can create a lasting negative impression in seconds. A positive first impression is so important; here are some suggestions to help you get off to a good start:

- **Dress and groom like the interviewer is likely to be dressed— but cleaner!** Employer surveys find that almost half of all people's dress or grooming create an initial negative impression. So this is a big problem. If necessary, get advice on your interviewing outfits from someone who dresses well. Pay close attention to your grooming, too. Little things do count.

(continued)

(continued)

- **Be early.** Leave home in plenty of time to be a few minutes early to an interview.

- **Be friendly and respectful with the receptionist.** Doing otherwise will often get back to the interviewer and result in a quick rejection.

- **Follow the interviewer's lead in the first few minutes.** It's often informal small talk, but it's very important for that person to see how you interact. This is a good time to make a positive comment on the organization or even something you see in the office.

- **Do some homework on the organization before you go.** You can often get information on a business and on industry trends from the Internet or a library.

- **Make a good impression before you arrive.** Your resume, e-mails, applications, and other written correspondence create an impression before the interview, so make them professional and error free.

Eight Important Actions for Interview Success

Although most people know that the interview is important to both you and the employer, few job seekers have a clear sense of what they need to accomplish during those critical minutes. Before I teach you interview techniques, I ask you to consider just what it is you want to accomplish in an interview. I believe the following eight actions are most important.

1. Make a Positive Impression

These tips can help you make a positive impression before and during your interview.

Before the Interview

What happens before the interview is extremely important, although it's often overlooked. Before you meet prospective employers, you often have indirect contact with those who know them. You might even contact the employer directly through e-mail, a phone call, or correspondence. Each of these contacts creates an impression.

There are three ways an interviewer may form an impression of you before meeting you face-to-face:

1. **The interviewer already knows you.** An employer may know you from previous contacts or from someone else's description of you. In this situation, your best approach is to acknowledge that relationship, but treat the interview in all other respects as a business meeting.

2. **You have contacted the interviewer through e-mail or by phone.** E-mail and the phone are important job search tools. How you handle these contacts creates an impression, even though the contacts are brief. For example, both contact via the phone and contact via e-mail give an impression of your language skills and ability to present yourself in a competent way; e-mail also quickly communicates your level of written communication skills. So if you set up an interview with the employer, you have already created an impression, most likely positive enough.

   You should call the day before the interview to verify the time of your meeting. Say something like: "Hi, I want to confirm that our interview for two o'clock tomorrow is still on." Get any directions you need. This kind of call is just another way of demonstrating your attention to detail and helps to communicate the importance you are placing on this interview.

   > **Tip:** Administrative assistants, receptionists, and other staff you have contact with may also mention their observations to the interviewer, so be professional and courteous in all encounters with staff.

3. **The interviewer has read your resume and other job search correspondence.** Prior to most interviews, you provide the employer with some sort of information or paperwork that creates an impression. Sending a note, letter, or e-mail beforehand often creates the impression that you are well-organized. Applications, resumes, and other correspondence sent or e-mailed in advance help the interviewer know more about you. If they are well done, they will help to create a positive impression. (For quick advice for putting together an effective resume, see *Same-Day Resume,* another book in the *Help in a Hurry* series.)

The Day of the Interview

To make a good impression on interview day, use these tips:

1. **Get there on time.** Try to schedule several interviews within the same area of town and time frame to avoid wasted time in excessive travel. Ask for directions from the receptionist or office manager and be sure you know how to get there and how long it will take. Allow plenty of time for traffic or other problems and plan on arriving for the interview 5 to 10 minutes early.

2. **Check your appearance.** Arrive early enough to slip into a restroom and correct any grooming problems your travel may have caused, such as wind-blown hair. You would be surprised how many people go into the interview with pen marks on their face or smudged lipstick on their teeth. Use a breath mint or gum just to be on the safe side. Do not spray on perfume, cologne, or hair spray right before the interview because many people are sensitive to chemicals and scents.

3. **Use appropriate waiting-room behavior.** As you wait for the interview to begin, keep in mind that it's important to relax and to look relaxed. Occupy yourself with something businesslike. For example, you could review your notes on questions you might like to ask in the interview, key skills you want to present, or other interview details. Bring a work-related magazine to read or pick up one in the reception area. The waiting room may also have publications from the organization itself that you may not have seen yet. You could also use this time to update your daily schedule.

4. **Be prepared if the interviewer is late.** Hope that it happens. If you arrive promptly but have to wait past the appointed time, that puts the interviewer in a "Gee, I'm sorry, I owe you one" frame of mind. If the interviewer is 15 minutes late, approach the office manager or administrative assistant and say something like: "I have an appointment to keep yet today. Do you think it will

> **Tip:** If you are a smoker, don't smoke during the interview because a nonsmoker is often seen as a more desirable worker. You may have other mannerisms that create negative impressions, too, such as slouching or cracking your knuckles or creating a mess by spreading out your coat and papers across the next seat. Avoid doing these things as well.

be much longer before (insert interviewer's name) will be free?" Be nice, but don't act as though you can sit around all day, either. If you have to wait more than 25 minutes beyond the scheduled time, ask to reschedule the interview at a better time. Say it is no problem for you and you understand things do come up. Besides, you say, you want to be sure Mr. or Ms. So-and-So doesn't feel rushed when he or she sees you. Set up the new time, accept any apology with a smile, and be on your way. When you do come back for your interview, the odds are that the interviewer will apologize—and treat you very well indeed.

5. **Be particular about your dress and appearance.** How you dress and groom can create a big negative or positive impression, especially during the first few seconds of an interview. With so many options in styles, colors, and other factors, determining the "correct" approach can get quite complex. To avoid the complexity, follow this simple rule: Dress and groom like the interviewer is likely to be dressed and groomed, but just a bit better (and cleaner!).

6. **Give a firm handshake and maintain good eye contact.** If the employer offers his or her hand, give a firm (but not too firm) handshake as you smile. As ridiculous as it sounds, a little practice helps. Avoid staring, but do look at the interviewer when either of you is speaking. It will help you concentrate on what is being said and indicate to the employer that you are listening closely and have good social skills.

7. **Act interested.** When you are sitting, lean slightly forward in your chair and keep your head up, looking directly at the interviewer. This stance helps you look interested and alert.

8. **Eliminate annoying behaviors.** Try to eliminate any distracting movements or mannerisms. A woman in one of my workshops saw herself in a videotape constantly playing with her hair. Only then did she realize that she had this distracting behavior. Listen to yourself and you may notice that you say "aaahhh" or "ummmmm" frequently, or say "you know what I mean?" over and over, or use other repetitive words or phrases. You may hardly be aware of doing this, but do watch for it. Ask friends or family for help pinpointing these behaviors.

9. **Pay attention to your voice.** If you are naturally soft-spoken, work on increasing your volume slightly. Listen to news announcers and

other professional speakers who are good models for volume, speed, and voice tone. I, for example, have a fairly deep voice. I have learned to change my intonation while doing presentations so that everyone doesn't go to sleep. Your voice and delivery will improve as you gain experience and conduct more interviews.

10. **Use the interviewer's formal name as often as possible.** Do this particularly in the early part of the interview and again when you are ending it. Do not call the interviewer by his or her first name unless the interviewer suggests otherwise.

11. **Play the chitchat game for awhile.** Interviewers often comment on the weather, ask if you had trouble getting there, or make some other common opening. Be friendly and make a few appropriate comments. Do not push your way into the business of your visit too early because these informal openings are standard measures of your socialization skills. Smile. It's nonverbal, and people will respond more favorably to you if you smile at them.

12. **Comment on something personal in the interviewer's office.** "I love your office! Did you decorate it yourself?" or "I noticed the sailboat. Do you sail?" or "Your office manager is great! How long has he been here?" The idea here is to express interest in something that interests the employer and encourage her or him to speak about it. This kind of interest is a compliment if your enthusiasm shows. This tactic can also provide you the opportunity to share something you have in common, so try to pick a topic you know something about.

13. **Ask some opening questions.** As soon as you have completed the necessary pleasant chitchat, be prepared to get the interview off in the direction you wish it to go. This process can happen within a minute of your first greeting, but is more likely to take up to five minutes. See the section later in this chapter titled "3. Use Control Statements to Your Advantage" for details on how to do this.

2. Communicate Your Skills

If you have created a reasonably positive image of yourself so far, an interviewer will now be interested in the specifics of why they should consider hiring you. This back-and-forth conversation usually lasts from 15 to 45 minutes and many consider it to be the most important and most difficult task in the entire job search.

Fortunately, by reading this book, you will have several advantages over the average job seeker:

1. You will know what sort of job you want.

2. You will know what skills are required to do well in that job.

3. You will have those very skills.

The only thing you have to do is to communicate these three things by directly and completely answering the questions an employer asks you. Chapter 1 helps you recognize your skills and communicate them to an interviewer.

3. Use Control Statements to Your Advantage

A *control statement* is a statement you make that becomes the roadmap for where the interview is going. Although you might think that you are at the mercy of the interviewer, you do have some ability to direct the interview from chitchat to the focus you desire.

For example, if this is a traditional interview, you might say something direct, such as "I'd like to tell you about what I've done, what I enjoy doing, and why I think it would be a good match with your organization." Your control statement can come at the beginning of the interview if things seem fuzzy after the chitchat or any time in the interview when you feel the focus is shifting away from the points you want to make.

Here are some control statements and questions to ask in informational and other nontraditional interviews:

- "How did you get started in this type of career?"

- "I'd like to know more about what your organization does. Would you mind telling me?"

- "I have a background in _____ and am interested in how I might be considered for a position in an organization such as yours."

- "I have three years of experience plus two years of training in the field of _____. I am actively looking for a job and know that you probably do not have openings now; but I would be interested in future openings. Perhaps if I told you a few things about myself, you could give me some idea of whether you would be interested in me."

4. Answer Problem Questions Well

All employers try to uncover problems or limitations you might bring to their job. Yet one survey of employers found that about 80 percent of job seekers cannot provide a good answer to one or more problem interview questions. Everyone has a problem of some sort, and the employer will try to find yours. Expect it. Suppose that you have been out of work for three months. That could be seen as a problem, unless you can provide a good reason for it. Later in this Step, I give pointers on a three-step process for answering any interview question well.

Top 10 Problem Interview Questions

Your answers to a few key problem questions may determine whether you get a job offer. There are simply too many possible interview questions to cover one by one. Instead, the 10 basic questions that follow cover variations of most other interview questions. So, if you can learn to answer these 10 questions well, you will know how to answer most others.

1. Why should I hire you?
2. Why don't you tell me about yourself?
3. What are your major strengths?
4. What are your major weaknesses?
5. What sort of pay do you expect to receive?
6. How does your previous experience relate to the jobs we have here?
7. What are your plans for the future?
8. What will your former employer (or references) say about you?
9. Why are you looking for this type of position, and why here?
10. Why don't you tell me about your personal situation?

5. Ask Key Questions

Many employers ask at some point in the interview whether you have any questions. How you respond affects their evaluation of you. So be prepared to ask insightful questions about the organization. Good topics to touch on include the following:

- The competitive environment in which the organization operates
- Executive management styles

- What obstacles the organization anticipates in meeting its goals

- How the organization's goals have changed over the past three to five years

Generally, asking about pay, benefits, or other similar topics at this time is unwise. The reason is that doing so tends to make you seem more interested in what the organization can do for you, rather than in what you can do for it. Having no questions at all makes you appear passive or disinterested, rather than curious and interested.

A Traditional Interview Is Not a Friendly Exchange

In a traditional interview situation, there is a job opening, and you will be one of several who've applied for it. In this setting, the employer's task is to eliminate all applicants but one. The interviewer's questions are designed to elicit information that can be used to screen you out. And your objective is to avoid getting screened out. It's hardly an open and honest interaction, is it?

This illustrates yet another advantage of setting up interviews before an opening exists. This eliminates the stress of a traditional interview. Employers are not trying to screen you out, and you are not trying to keep them from finding out stuff about you.

---

6. Help Employers Know Why They Should Hire You

Even if the interviewer never directly says it, the question in his or her mind is always "Why should I hire you?" The best response to this question provides advantages to the employer, not to you. A good response provides proof that you can help an employer make more money by improving efficiency, reducing costs, increasing sales, or solving problems (by coming to work on time, improving customer service, organizing one or more operations, offering knowledge of a particular software or computer system, or a variety of other things).

> ### *The Most Important Interview Question of All:*
> ### *"Why Should I Hire You?"*
>
> This is the most important question to answer well. Do you have a convincing argument why someone should hire you over someone else? If you don't, you probably won't get that job you really want. So think carefully about why someone should hire you and practice your response. Then make sure you communicate this in the interview, even if the interviewer never asks the question in a clear way.

7. Close the Interview Properly

As the interview comes to an end, remember these few things:

- **Don't let the interview last too long.** Most interviews last 30 to 60 minutes. Unless the interviewer asks otherwise, plan on staying no longer than an hour. Watch for hints from interviewers, such as looking at a watch or rustling papers, that indicate that they are ready to end the interview.

- **Summarize the key points of the interview.** Use your judgment here and keep it short! Review the major issues that came up in the interview with the employer. You can skip this step if time is short.

- **If a problem came up, repeat your resolution of it.** Whatever you think that particular interviewer may see as a reason not to hire you, bring it up again and present your reasons why you don't see it as a problem. If you are not sure what the interviewer is thinking, be direct and ask, "Is there anything about me that concerns you or might keep you from hiring me?" Whatever comes up, do as well as you can in responding to it.

- **Review your strengths for this job.** This is another chance for you to present the skills you possess that relate to this particular job. Emphasize your key strengths only and keep your statements brief.

- **If you want the job, ask for it.** If you want the job, say so and explain why. Employers are more willing to hire someone they know is excited about the job, so let them know if you are. Ask when you can start. This question may not always be appropriate, but if it is, do it.

The Call-Back Close

This interview-closing approach requires some courage, but it does work. Practice it a few times and use it in your early interviews to get more comfortable with it.

1. **Thank the interviewer by name.** While shaking their hand, say, "Thank you (Mr. or Mrs. or Ms. _____) for your time today."

2. **Express interest.** Depending on the situation, express your interest in the job, organization, service, or product by saying, "I'm very interested in the ideas we went over today," or "I'm very interested in your organization. It seems to be an exciting place to work." Or, if a job opening exists and you want it, confidently say, "I am definitely interested in this position."

3. **Mention your busy schedule.** Say "I'm busy for the next few days, but..."

4. **Arrange a reason and a time to call back.** Your objective is to leave a reason for you to get back in touch and to arrange for a specific day and time to do so. For example, say, "I'm sure I'll have questions. When would be the best time for me to get back with you?" Notice that I said "When" rather than "Is it okay to..." because asking when does not easily allow a "no" response. Get a specific day and a best time to call.

5. **Say good-bye.**

8. Follow Up After the Interview

Following up can make the difference between being unemployed or underemployed and getting the job you want fast. When you get home from the interview, do the following:

- **Make notes on the interview.** While it is fresh in your mind, jot down key points. A week later, you may not remember something essential.

- **Schedule your follow-up.** If you agreed to call back next Monday between 9:00 a.m. and 10:00 a.m., you are likely to forget unless you put it on your schedule.

- **Send your thank-you note.** Send the note the very same day if possible. Send an e-mail thank-you that day, and follow this with a thank-you note through regular mail.

- **Call when you said you would!** When you call when you said you would, you create the impression of being organized and wanting the job. If you do have a specific question, ask it at this time. If a job opening exists and you do want it, say that you want it and explain why. If no job opening exists, say you enjoyed the visit and would like to stay in touch during your job search. If interviewers referred you to others, let them know how these contacts went. Ask them what they suggest your next step should be. This would also be a good time to ask, if you have not done so before, for the names of anyone else with whom you might speak about a position for a person with your skills and experience. Then, of course, follow up with any new referrals.

- **Schedule more follow-up.** Set a time to talk with this person again. And, of course, send the interviewer another thank-you note or e-mail.

The Three-Step Process for Answering Most Interview Questions

There are thousands of questions that you could be asked in an interview, and there is no way you can memorize a "correct" response for each one—especially not the night before the interview. Interviews just aren't like that because they are often conversational and informal. The unexpected often happens. For these reasons, developing an *approach* to answering an interview question is far more important than memorizing a canned response.

I have developed a technique called the Three-Step Process that you can use to fashion an effective answer to most interview questions:

1. **Understand what is really being asked.** Most questions relate to your adaptive skills and personality. These questions include "Can we depend on you?"; "Are you easy to get along with?"; and "Are you a good worker?" The question may also relate to whether you have the experience and training to do the job if you are hired.

2. **Answer the question briefly in a nondamaging way.** A good response to a question should acknowledge the facts of your situation and present them as an advantage rather than a disadvantage.

3. **Answer the real question by presenting your related skills.** An effective response to any interview question should answer the question in a direct way that also presents your ability to do the job well.

To show you how to use the Three-Step Process, let's use it to answer a specific question:

> **Question:** "We were looking for someone with more experience in this field than you seem to have. Why should we consider you over others with better credentials?"

The following sections show how one person might construct an answer to this question using the Three-Step Process.

Step 1: Understand What Is Really Being Asked

This question is often asked in a less direct way, but it is a frequent concern of employers. To answer it, you must remember that employers often hire people who present themselves well in an interview over those with better credentials. Your best shot is to emphasize whatever personal strengths you have that could offer an advantage to an employer. The person wants to know whether you have anything going for you that can help you compete with a more experienced worker.

Well, do you? Are you a hard worker? Do you learn fast? Have you had intensive training or hands-on experience? Do you have skills from other activities that can transfer to this job? Knowing in advance what skills you have to offer is essential to answering this question.

Step 2: Answer the Question Briefly in a Nondamaging Way

For example, the following response answers the question without hurting the person's chances of getting the job:

> "I'm sure there are people who have more years of experience or better credentials. I do, however, have four years of combined training and hands-on experience using the latest methods and techniques. Because my training is recent, I am open to new ideas and am used to working hard and learning quickly."

Step 3: Answer the Real Question by Presenting Your Related Skills

Although the previous response answers the question in an appropriate and brief way, you might continue with additional details that emphasize key skills needed for the job:

> "As you know, I held down a full-time job and family responsibilities while going to school. During those two years, I had an excellent attendance record both at work and school, missing only one day in two years. I also received two merit increases in salary, and my grades were in the top 25 percent of my class. In order to do all this, I had to learn to organize my time and set priorities. I worked hard to prepare myself in this new career area and am willing to keep working to establish myself. The position you have available is what I am prepared to do. I am willing to work harder than the next person because I have the desire to keep learning and to do an outstanding job. With my education complete, I can now turn my full attention to this job."

This response presents the skills necessary to do well in any job. This job seeker sounds dependable. She also gave examples of situations where she had used the required skills in other settings.

The Prove-It Technique

The Three-Step Process is important for understanding that the interview question being asked is often an attempt to discover underlying information. You can provide that information in an effective way by using the four-step Prove-It Technique:

1. **Present a concrete example:** People relate to and remember stories. Saying you have a skill is not nearly as powerful as describing a situation where you used that skill. The example should include enough details to make sense of the who, what, where, when, and why.

2. **Quantify:** Whenever possible, use numbers to provide a basis for what you did. For example, give the number of customers served, the percent you exceeded quotas, dollar amounts you were responsible for, or the number of new accounts you generated.

3. **Emphasize results:** Providing some data regarding the positive results you obtained is important. For example, someone could state that sales increased by 3 percent over the previous year or profits went up 50 percent. Use numbers to quantify your results.

4. **Link it up:** Although the connection between your example and doing the job well may seem obvious to you, make sure it is clear to the employer. A simple statement is often enough to accomplish this.

If you do a thorough job of completing the activities in chapter 1, providing proof supporting the skills you discuss in an interview should be fairly easy.

Negotiating Salary

Most people don't negotiate their salaries, partly because few know how to negotiate effectively. At one time or another, each of us has failed at this process. Most job seekers accept the first offer thrown their way because they're afraid that negotiating will kill any chances to get the job. I personally never attempted to negotiate a salary package during the early years of my career because nodding politely and saying, "That's fine" was the path of least resistance. But in today's economy, that passive acceptance can cost us more than we can afford to lose.

Four Strategic Negotiation Mistakes to Avoid

Negotiation experts cite four strategic mistakes that novice negotiators often make. Although these mistakes refer to negotiations in general, they are often at the root of salary negotiation problems as well.

1. **Lack of persistence.** Herb Cohen, author of *You Can Negotiate Anything,* told *USAir* magazine, "People present something to the other side, and if the other side doesn't 'buy' it right away, they shrug and move on to something else. If that's a quality you have, I suggest you change it. Learn to hang in there. You must be tenacious."

2. **Impatience.** As Michael Schatzki warns, "The impatient negotiator has two strikes against him. He's not willing to let the process work itself out, and he's not willing to be deadlocked for a while and see what happens. And time often is the key to successfully concluding a negotiation."

3. **Going in too low.** All too often one side in the negotiation process accepts in advance a settlement that is lower than the other side had in mind. Once a low position is revealed, an experienced negotiator is unlikely to go higher.

4. **Lack of research.** Few people are prepared with facts to back up their position in negotiations. They go on "feel" to establish a value. Lack of preparation can be a very expensive mistake.

Farr's Four Rules of Salary Negotiation

The following four sections describe some basic rules of salary negotiation that you should keep in mind.

Early Pay Discussions Can Screen You Out

Early in the traditional screening process, many employers want to know how much you expect to be paid. Before the interview, they may seek this information on applications and in want ads. And some employers ask you how much you expect to earn very early in the interview process.

Just why is this information so important to them? The reason is that many employers don't want to waste their time with people who have salary expectations far above what they are willing to pay. Put simply, they want the information so that they can screen you out.

Employers look for ways to eliminate as many people as possible during the early phases of a traditional interview process. There may be many applicants for an opening, particularly if the job was advertised or is reasonably attractive in some way. Employers will try to find out whether you want more money than they are willing to pay. If so, they figure that, if hired, you may soon leave for a better-paying job. That is the reason for my first rule regarding salary negotiations.

Farr's Salary Negotiation Rule #1
Never talk money until after an employer decides he or she wants you.

Discussing salary early in the interviewing process is not to your advantage. Your best position is to use techniques that are likely to satisfy a curious employer without giving a specific dollar amount. Here are a few ways you could respond to an initial interview inquiry about your pay expectations:

- "What salary range do you pay for positions with similar requirements?"

- "I'm very interested in the position, and my salary would be negotiable."

- "Tell me what you have in mind for the salary range."

- "I am interested in the job and would consider any reasonable offer you might make."

"Employers are anxious to know how your joining the organization will impact their bottom line, and they'll try to get to the subject as soon as possible," says Doug Matthews, Executive Vice President of Career Transition Services for Right Management Associates, an executive outplacement firm. Salary issues are the main reasons candidates are knocked out of the running during the screening process, according to outplacement industry surveys. Responding appropriately to salary questions can get you past screening interviewers, who rarely have authority to negotiate salaries, and in front of decision-makers with whom the real negotiations take place.

So always defer the question as many times as you have to until you are sure it's the real thing and not just part of a screening process. Then, when the timing is right, maneuver the interviewer into naming the starting point. Just remember the most important rule of salary negotiations: The one who speaks first loses.

With a bit of luck, stall tactics such as these will get the employer to tell you the salary range or at least delay further discussion until later, when it matters. If that doesn't work and the employer still insists on knowing your salary expectations, there are still some things you can do.

Know the Probable Salary Range in Advance

Approaching an interview without being prepared for discussions of pay is not wise. Although you will have to do a bit of research, knowing what an employer is likely to pay is essential in salary negotiations.

Farr's Salary Negotiation Rule #2

Know in advance the probable salary range for similar jobs in similar organizations.

The trick is to think in terms of a wide *range* in salary, rather than a particular number. Keep in mind that larger organizations tend to pay more than smaller ones, and various areas of the country differ greatly in pay scales. Find out the general range that jobs of this sort are likely to pay in your area. That information is relatively easy to obtain; all it may take is asking those who work in similar jobs or visiting the library.

Bracket the Salary Range

Let's assume that you have done your homework and you know a range that you are likely to be offered for a given job in your area. And let's also assume that you run into an interviewer who insists on knowing how much you expect to be paid. If this happens, I suggest negotiation rule #3.

Farr's Salary Negotiation Rule #3

Always bracket your stated salary range to begin within the employer's probable salary range and end a bit above what you expect to settle for.

Even if you have a good idea of how much a job might pay, you can easily get trapped into making a very costly mistake. Suppose that the employer is expecting to pay someone about $25,000 a year. Your research indicates that most jobs of this type pay between $22,000 and $29,000 a year. Let's also assume that you have run into an interviewer who insists on you revealing your pay expectations in the first interview.

You want to be a clever negotiator, so you say you were hoping for $30,000. You figure that stating that number will make the interviewer think you are not an easy target and will encourage him or her to make a higher offer later. Wrong. In many cases, saying this amount will probably eliminate you from consideration.

If you say you would take $22,000, one of two things could happen:

1. You could get hired at $22,000 a year, probably making that response the most expensive two seconds in your entire life.

2. The employer could look for someone else, because you must be worth only $22,000, and he or she wants someone who is worth more.

Once again, questions about pay during the early phases of the interviewing process are designed to help the employer either eliminate you from consideration or save money at your expense. You could get lucky and name the salary they had in mind, but the stakes are too high for me to recommend that approach. Your best bet is to be informed.

In my example, you figured that the probable range for the salary would be from $22,000 to $29,000. That is a wide range, but you could cover it by saying

"I was looking for a salary in the mid- to upper twenties."

This response avoids mentioning a specific salary, and it covers a wide range.

If you were an employer and someone responded this way, how might you react? Most employers take a moment to consider the response and, after doing so, often conclude that your range is the same one that they are considering. The particular number the firm has in mind just happens to be $25,000, and your response "brackets" that figure. The impasse is over, and you can both get on with the interview. You win, and they don't lose.

Talking in terms of a salary range that extends a bit above what the employer was likely to consider often results in one of two positive outcomes:

1. If you are offered the job, you are likely to be offered more than the employer may have originally been willing to consider.

2. It gives you the option of negotiating your salary when it matters most—when the employer has offered you a job.

Don't Say No Too Soon

Too often, people lose the ability to negotiate salary because they mishandle the offer or its discussion. This brings me to rule #4:

> ### *Farr's Salary Negotiation Rule #4*
> Never say no to a job offer either before it is made or within 24 hours afterward.

Never, never turn down a job offer in an interview! Let's say that you get a job offer at half the salary you expected. Avoid the temptation to turn it down there and then. Instead, say:

> "Thank you for your offer. I am flattered that you think I can do the job. Because this decision is so important to me, I would like to consider your offer and get back with you within two days."

Leave and see if you change your mind. If not, call back and say, in effect:

> "I've given your offer considerable thought and feel that I just can't take it at the salary you've offered. Is there any way that I could be paid more, in the range of _____?"

Even as you say no, leave the door open to keep negotiating. If the employer wants you, he or she may be willing to meet your terms. It happens more than you might imagine. If the employer cannot meet your salary needs, say thank you again, and let him or her know you are interested in future openings within your salary range. Then stay in touch. You never know.

> **Tip:** *Do not reject a job offer to try to get a higher wage. Understand that once you reject an offer, the deal is off. You must be willing to lose that job forever.*

Accepting the Offer

Just as you shouldn't reject an offer too quickly, take time to think about accepting a job, too. Accepting a reasonable offer right away can be a mistake. Germann and Arnold list the following considerations that many people ignore in the rush to accept or reject a job offer:

- Is the job description (duties, responsibilities, and authority) clear?

- What is the employer's attitude toward advancement?

- Who will you be working with?

If you don't have a straight answer yet for these questions, don't make a move you could regret. Instead, keep plugging away until the picture comes into clear focus.

Also, discussing the offer with others before saying yes is often wise. Here is one way to delay until you can give the offer some thought:

> "Thank you for the offer. The position is very much what I wanted in many ways, and I am delighted at your interest. This decision is an important one for me, and I would like some time to consider your offer."

Ask for 24 hours to consider your decision and, when calling back, consider negotiating for something reasonable. A bit more money, every other Tuesday afternoon off, or some other benefit would be nice if you can get it easily. However, if you want the job, do not jeopardize obtaining it with unreasonable demands. If your request causes a problem, make it very clear that you want the job anyway.

Key Points: Step 6

- The most important actions for interview success are to make a good impression, communicate your skills, use control statements, answer problem questions well, ask key questions, help the employer know why he or she should hire you, close the interview properly, and follow up after the interview.

- You can answer almost any interview question by using a simple Three-Step Process.

- Remember Farr's Four Rules of Salary Negotiation: Don't talk salary too early; know the probable salary range for the job in advance; bracket the salary range; and don't say no too soon.

Follow Up on All Job Leads

It's a fact: People who follow up with potential employers and with others in their network get jobs faster than those who do not. Here are four rules to guide you as you follow up in your job search:

1. Send a thank-you note or e-mail to every person who helps you in your job search.

2. Send the note within 24 hours after speaking with the person.

3. Enclose JIST Cards in thank-you notes and all other correspondence.

4. Develop a system to keep following up with good contacts.

This chapter gives details on how to follow up with your contacts most effectively.

Thank-You Notes Make a Difference

Be sure to send a thank-you note within 24 hours of every job interview or networking contact you have. It's a common courtesy to show appreciation for someone's help; however, many people don't make the effort to do so. If you are prompt with your notes, you will stand out from the crowd of other job seekers.

Although thank-you notes can be e-mailed, most people appreciate and are more impressed by a mailed note. Here are some tips about mailed thank-you notes that you can easily adapt to e-mail use:

- Thank-you notes can be handwritten or typed on quality paper and matching envelopes.

- Keep them simple, neat, and error free.

- Make sure to include a few copies of your JIST Card (see chapter 3 for details on how to create JIST Cards).

An example of a simple thank-you note follows.

April 5, XXXX

Ms. Kijek,

Thanks so much for your willingness to see me next Wednesday at 9 a.m. I know that I am one of many who are interested in working with your organization. I appreciate the opportunity to meet you and learn more about the position.

I've enclosed a JIST Card that presents the basics of my skills for this job and will bring my resume to the interview. Please call me if you have any questions at all.

Sincerely,

Bruce Vernon

Figure 7-1: A sample thank-you note.

Develop an Organized System for Following Up

If you use contact-management software, use it to schedule follow-up activities. Pocket schedulers and organizers can also be very helpful to remind you of interviews and things to do. A simple paper system, such as a planner notebook, can work very well also; or you can adapt it for setting up your contact management software.

Following are a few ideas for setting up your follow-up system.

Use Job Lead Cards

By using the job search methods you have learned in this book, you can develop hundreds of contacts. Keeping track of them is more than any person's memory can handle.

Look at the sample job lead card in figure 7-2. It shows the kind of information you can keep about each person who helps you in your job search. (If you want, you can list the same kind of information in a computer database.)

To start such a system, buy a few hundred 3-by-5–inch cards. Create one job lead card for every person who gives you a referral or who is a possible employer. Keep brief notes each time you talk with that person, to help you remember important details for your next contact. Notice that the notes on the sample card are short, but they contain enough data to help the job seeker remember what happened and when to follow up.

ORGANIZATION: _Mutual Health Insurance_

CONTACT PERSON: _Anna Tomey_   PHONE: _317-355-0216_

SOURCE OF LEAD: _Aunt Ruth_

NOTES: _4/10 Called. Anna on vacation. Call back 4/15. 4/15 Interview set 4/20 at 1:30. 4/20 Anna showed me around. They use the same computers we used in school! (Friendly people.) Sent thank-you note and JIST Card, call back 5/1. 5/1 Second interview 5/8 at 9 a.m.!_

Figure 7-2: A sample job lead card.

Maintain a Job Search Follow-Up Box

As you contact more and more people in your job search, the number of job lead cards you create for future follow-up will increase. You will get more and more new leads as you follow up with people you've contacted one or more times in the past. You need a way to organize all those job lead cards.

Most department and office-supply stores sell small file boxes for 3-by-5–inch cards, as well as tabbed dividers for these boxes. Everything you need will cost about $10.

Set up file box dividers for each day of the month, numbering them 1 through 31. Then, file each completed job lead card under the date when you want to follow up on it.

Every Monday, simply review all the job lead cards you have filed for the week. On your weekly schedule, list any interviews or follow-up calls you promised to make at a particular date and time. At the start of each day, pull the job lead cards filed under that date. List appointments and calls on your Daily Job Search Contact Sheet (described in the next section).

Keep Trying

Here are some other ways you can use this simple follow-up system to get results:

- You get the name of a person to call, but you can't reach this person right away. Create a job lead card and file it under tomorrow's date.

- You call someone from a yellow pages listing, but she is busy this week. She asks you to call back in two weeks. You file this job lead card under the date for two weeks in the future.

- You get an interview with a person who doesn't have any openings now. He gives you the name of someone who might have an opening. After you send a thank-you note and JIST Card to the original contact, you file his name under a date a few weeks in the future, so that you can check for any future openings.

Following up with past contacts is one of the most effective ways of getting a job. The job search follow-up box is a simple, inexpensive system that works very well. You can do the same thing with computer scheduling software, but it doesn't work any better than the box.

Make a Daily Job Search Contact Sheet

If you do what I suggest, you will try each day to set up two interviews. To get this done, you will have to contact a lot of people. Some you will contact for the first time; others you will follow up with from earlier contacts.

To get you started, I suggest that you begin each day by completing a Daily Job Search Contact Sheet. Use it to list at least 20 people or organizations to call. Use any sources to get these leads, including people you know, referrals, yellow pages leads, Internet leads, and want ads. An example of a contact sheet follows.

SAMPLE DAILY JOB SEARCH CONTACT SHEET

Contact Name/ Organization	Referral Source	Job Lead Card?	Phone Number/ E-mail Address
1. Manager/The Flower Show	Yellow pages	Yes	897-6041
2. Manager/Rainbow Flowers	Listed on Rainbow's Web site	Yes	admin@rainbowflowers.com
3. Joyce Wilson/Hartley Nurseries	John Lee	Yes	892-2224
4. John Mullahy/Roses, Etc.	Uncle Jim	Yes	299-4226
5. None/Plants to Go	Want Ad	Yes	835-7016

Figure 7-3: The daily job search contact sheet.

Is a Computer or PDA Better than 3-by-5 Cards?

Maybe not. If you already use scheduling or time-management software or a PDA (personal digital assistant, like a PALM), go ahead and use it to manage your job search contacts. If you don't use such software now, you will probably be better off trying the card system I suggest. The reason is simple— it works. Instead of spending your time messing with new software, you can go right to work making contacts and getting results.

Key Points: Step 7

- Send an e-mail or handwritten thank-you note within 24 hours of an interview or other networking contact.

- Develop an organized system for following up on job leads that can include job lead cards, a file box, and a Daily Job Search Contact Sheet; or an electronic scheduler.

In Closing

This is a short book, but it may be all you need to get a better job in less time. I hope this will be true for you and wish you well in your search.

Do remember that nobody is going to knock on your door and offer you a job. Job seeking does involve luck, but you are more likely to get lucky if you are out getting interviews.

I'll close this book with a few final tips:

- **Approach your job search as if it were a job itself.** Create and stick to a daily schedule, and spend at least 25 hours a week looking.

- **Follow up on each lead you generate and ask each contact for referrals.**

- **Set out each day to schedule at least two interviews.** Remember the new definition of an interview, which includes talking to businesses that don't have an opening now.

- **Send out lots of thank-you notes and JIST Cards.**

- **When you want the job, tell the employer that you want it and why the company should hire you over someone else.**

Don't get discouraged. There are lots of jobs out there, and someone needs an employee with your skills—your job is to find that someone.

I wish you luck in your job search and in your life.

Appendix A

The Essential Job Search Data Worksheet

Take some time to complete this worksheet carefully. It will help you write your resume and answer interview questions. You can also tear it out and take it with you to help complete applications and as a reference throughout your job search.

Use an erasable pen or pencil to allow for corrections. Whenever possible, emphasize skills and accomplishments that support your ability to do the job you want. Use extra sheets as needed.

ESSENTIAL JOB SEARCH DATA WORKSHEET

Your name _____

Date completed _____

Job objective _____

_____

_____

Key Accomplishments

List three accomplishments that best prove your ability to do the kind of job you want.

1. _____

2. _____

3. _____

(continued)

(continued)

Education and Training

Name of high school(s); years attended_____

_____

_____

Subjects related to job objective_____

_____

_____

_____

_____

Related extracurricular activities/hobbies/leisure activities_____

_____

_____

_____

_____

Accomplishments/things you did well_____

_____

_____

_____

_____

Specific things you can do as a result_____

_____

_____

_____

_____

Schools you attended after high school; years attended; degrees/certificates earned _____

_____

_____

_____

_____

Courses related to job objective _____

_____

_____

_____

_____

Related extracurricular activities/hobbies/leisure activities _____

_____

_____

_____

_____

Accomplishments/things you did well _____

_____

_____

_____

_____

Specific things you can do as a result _____

_____

_____

_____

_____

(continued)

(continued)

Other Training

Include formal or informal learning, workshops, military training, things you learned on the job or from hobbies—anything that will help support your job objective. Include specific dates, certificates earned, or other details as needed. _____

_____

_____

_____

_____

Work and Volunteer History

List your most recent job first, followed by each previous job. Military experience, unpaid or volunteer work, and work in a family business should be included here, too. If needed, use additional sheets to cover *all* significant paid or unpaid work experiences.

Emphasize details that will help support your new job objective. Include numbers to support what you did: number of people served over one or more years, number of transactions processed, percentage of sales increased, total inventory value you were responsible for, payroll of the staff you supervised, total budget responsible for, and so on.

Emphasize results you achieved, using numbers to support them whenever possible. Mentioning these things on your resume and in an interview will help you get the job you want.

Job 1

Dates employed _____

_____

Name of organization _____

_____

Supervisor's name and job title_____

_____

Address_____

_____

_____

_____

Phone number/e-mail address/Web site_____

_____

_____

What did you accomplish and do well?_____

_____

_____

_____

Things you learned; skills you developed or used_____

_____

_____

_____

Raises, promotions, positive evaluations, awards_____

_____

_____

_____

_____

Computer software, hardware, and other equipment you used

_____

_____

_____

_____

(continued)

(continued)

Other details that might support your job objective_____

_____

_____

_____

_____

Job 2

Dates employed _____

_____

Name of organization_____

_____

Supervisor's name and job title_____

_____

Address_____

_____

_____

_____

Phone number/e-mail address/Web site_____

_____

_____

What did you accomplish and do well?_____

_____

_____

_____

_____

Things you learned; skills you developed or used_____

_____

_____

_____

_____

Raises, promotions, positive evaluations, awards_____

_____

_____

_____

_____

Computer software, hardware, and other equipment you used

_____

_____

_____

_____

Other details that might support your job objective_____

_____

_____

_____

_____

Job 3

Dates employed_____

_____

Name of organization_____

_____

Supervisor's name and job title_____

_____

(continued)

Address _____

_____

_____

_____

Phone number/e-mail address/Web site _____

_____

_____

What did you accomplish and do well? _____

_____

_____

_____

_____

Things you learned; skills you developed or used _____

_____

_____

_____

_____

Raises, promotions, positive evaluations, awards _____

_____

_____

_____

Computer software, hardware, and other equipment you used

_____

_____

_____

_____

Other details that might support your job objective⎯⎯⎯⎯

⎯⎯⎯⎯⎯⎯⎯⎯⎯⎯⎯⎯⎯⎯⎯⎯⎯⎯⎯⎯⎯⎯⎯

⎯⎯⎯⎯⎯⎯⎯⎯⎯⎯⎯⎯⎯⎯⎯⎯⎯⎯⎯⎯⎯⎯⎯

⎯⎯⎯⎯⎯⎯⎯⎯⎯⎯⎯⎯⎯⎯⎯⎯⎯⎯⎯⎯⎯⎯⎯

⎯⎯⎯⎯⎯⎯⎯⎯⎯⎯⎯⎯⎯⎯⎯⎯⎯⎯⎯⎯⎯⎯⎯

References

Think of people who know your work well and will say positive things about your work and character. Past supervisors are best.

Contact them and tell them what type of job you want and your qualifications, and ask what they will say about you if contacted by a potential employer. Some employers will not provide references by phone, so ask them for a letter of reference in advance.

If a past employer may say negative things, negotiate what they will say or get written references from others you worked with there.

Reference name⎯⎯⎯⎯⎯⎯⎯⎯⎯⎯⎯⎯⎯⎯⎯

⎯⎯⎯⎯⎯⎯⎯⎯⎯⎯⎯⎯⎯⎯⎯⎯⎯⎯⎯⎯⎯⎯⎯

Position or title⎯⎯⎯⎯⎯⎯⎯⎯⎯⎯⎯⎯⎯⎯⎯⎯

⎯⎯⎯⎯⎯⎯⎯⎯⎯⎯⎯⎯⎯⎯⎯⎯⎯⎯⎯⎯⎯⎯⎯

Relationship to you⎯⎯⎯⎯⎯⎯⎯⎯⎯⎯⎯⎯⎯⎯

⎯⎯⎯⎯⎯⎯⎯⎯⎯⎯⎯⎯⎯⎯⎯⎯⎯⎯⎯⎯⎯⎯⎯

Contact information (complete address, phone number, e-mail address)⎯⎯⎯⎯⎯⎯⎯⎯⎯⎯⎯⎯⎯⎯⎯⎯⎯⎯⎯

⎯⎯⎯⎯⎯⎯⎯⎯⎯⎯⎯⎯⎯⎯⎯⎯⎯⎯⎯⎯⎯⎯⎯

⎯⎯⎯⎯⎯⎯⎯⎯⎯⎯⎯⎯⎯⎯⎯⎯⎯⎯⎯⎯⎯⎯⎯

⎯⎯⎯⎯⎯⎯⎯⎯⎯⎯⎯⎯⎯⎯⎯⎯⎯⎯⎯⎯⎯⎯⎯

Reference name⎯⎯⎯⎯⎯⎯⎯⎯⎯⎯⎯⎯⎯⎯⎯

⎯⎯⎯⎯⎯⎯⎯⎯⎯⎯⎯⎯⎯⎯⎯⎯⎯⎯⎯⎯⎯⎯⎯

(continued)

(continued)

Position or title _____

_____

Relationship to you _____

_____

Contact information (complete address, phone number, e-mail address) _____

_____

_____

_____

_____

Reference name _____

_____

Position or title _____

_____

Relationship to you _____

_____

Contact information (complete address, phone number, e-mail address) _____

_____

_____

_____

_____

Sample Job Description from the *Occupational Outlook Handbook*

What follows is one of the more than 270 job descriptions in the *Occupational Outlook Handbook (OOH)*, the most widely used source of job information in the U.S. To help you use the *OOH* most efficiently to find information about jobs that interest you, I have added boxes that list the many job-related questions you will find answers to in each section.

Some Tips for Using the *OOH* Job Descriptions in Your Job Search

- **Explore careers:** If you are changing careers or not sure of the job you want, identify jobs that interest you in the *OOH* table of contents. Then carefully read these descriptions to better understand which jobs best fit your current needs.

- **Identify alternative job targets:** Most job seekers overlook job opportunities because they are simply not familiar with them. But your past experience and transferable skills will often be enough to get you considered for a variety of jobs, including some with higher pay or other advantages. So spend some time browsing other *OOH* jobs that you might apply for during your job search.

- **Identify key skills to emphasize in the interview:** I've underlined some of the key skills in the sample job description that follows (see page 164). You can do something similar for your target job and then emphasize these skills in interviews. Pay particular attention to skills you have that match what the job requires. If you are weak in one or more of the key skills required, emphasize transferable skills you have that will help you acquire the skills you lack now.

- **Improve your resume:** In a similar way, you can review the *OOH* job descriptions to identify key skills a job requires and then emphasize those in your resume.

- **Negotiating pay and benefits:** The *OOH* gives information on the national average pay for a job, but keep in mind that some earn more and others earn less. Those with less experience typically earn less, and local pay may differ significantly from the pay rates presented in the *OOH.* So review the *OOH,* but also research local pay ranges for similar positions to prepare for more effective salary negotiations.

Sample Job Description from the *Occupational Outlook Handbook*

Accountants and Auditors

(O*NET 13-2011.01 and 13-2011.02)

Significant Points

> *Questions Answered in This Section:*
> - What are the most important things to know about this job?

- Most jobs require at least a bachelor's degree in accounting or a related field.

- Overall job opportunities should be favorable, although job seekers who obtain professional recognition through certification or licensure, a master's degree, proficiency in accounting and auditing computer software, or specialized expertise will have an advantage.

- An increase in the number of businesses, changing financial laws and regulations, and increased scrutiny of company finances will drive growth of accountants and auditors.

Nature of the Work

Questions Answered in This Section:

- What is this job like?

- What would I do on a daily basis in this job?

- What tools and equipment would I use on this job?

- How closely would I be supervised on this job?

- What are some alternative titles for this job?

- What are some of the specialties within this job?

Accountants and auditors help to ensure that the nation's firms are run efficiently, its public records kept accurately, and its taxes paid properly and on time. They perform these vital functions by offering an increasingly wide array of business and accounting services to their clients. These services include public, management, and government accounting, as well as internal auditing. Beyond the fundamental tasks of the occupation—preparing, analyzing, and verifying financial documents in order to provide information to clients—many accountants now are required to possess a wide range of knowledge and skills. Accountants and auditors are broadening the services they offer to include budget analysis, financial and investment planning, information technology consulting, and limited legal services.

Specific job duties vary widely among the four major fields of accounting: *public, management, government, and internal.*

Public accountants perform a broad range of accounting, auditing, tax, and consulting activities for their clients, who may be corporations, governments, nonprofit organizations, or individuals. For example, some public accountants concentrate on tax matters, such as advising companies of the tax advantages and disadvantages of certain business decisions and preparing individual income tax returns. Others offer advice in areas such as compensation or employee healthcare benefits, the design of accounting and data-processing systems, and the selection of controls to safeguard assets. Still others audit clients' financial statements and report to investors and authorities that the statements have been correctly prepared and reported. Public accountants, many of whom are Certified Public Accountants (CPAs), generally have their own businesses or work for public accounting firms.

Some public accountants specialize in forensic accounting—investigating and interpreting white-collar crimes such as securities fraud and embezzlement, bankruptcies and contract disputes, and other complex and possibly criminal financial transactions, such as money laundering by organized criminals. Forensic accountants combine their knowledge of accounting and finance with law and investigative techniques in order to determine if illegal activity is going on. Many forensic accountants work closely with law enforcement personnel and lawyers during investigations and often appear as expert witnesses during trials.

In response to the recent accounting scandals, new federal legislation restricts the nonauditing services that public accountants can provide to clients. If an accounting firm audits a client's financial statements, that same firm cannot provide advice in the areas of human resources, technology, investment banking, or legal matters, although accountants may still advise on tax issues, such as establishing a tax shelter. Accountants may still advise other clients in these areas, or may provide advice within their own firm.

Management accountants—also called cost, managerial, industrial, corporate, or private accountants—record and analyze the financial information of the companies for which they work. Other responsibilities include budgeting, performance evaluation, cost management, and asset management. Usually, management accountants are part of executive teams involved in strategic planning or new-product development. They analyze and interpret the financial information that corporate executives need to make sound business decisions. They also prepare financial reports for nonmanagement groups, including stockholders, creditors, regulatory agencies, and tax authorities. Within accounting departments, they may work in various areas, including financial analysis, planning and budgeting, and cost accounting.

Government accountants and auditors work in the public sector, maintaining and examining the records of government agencies and auditing private businesses and individuals whose activities are subject to government regulations or taxation. Accountants employed by federal, state, and local governments guarantee that revenues are received and expenditures are made in accordance with laws and regulations. Those who are employed by the federal government may work as Internal Revenue Service agents or in financial management, financial institution examination, or budget analysis and administration.

Internal auditors verify the accuracy of their organizations' internal records and check for mismanagement, waste, or fraud. Internal auditing is an increasingly important area of accounting and auditing. Internal auditors examine and evaluate their firm's financial and information systems, management procedures, and internal controls to ensure that records are accurate and controls are adequate to protect against fraud and waste. They also review company operations—evaluating their efficiency, effectiveness, and compliance with corporate policies and procedures, laws, and government regulations. There are many types of highly specialized auditors, such as electronic data-processing, environmental, engineering, legal, insurance premium, bank, and healthcare auditors. As computer systems make information timelier, internal auditors help managers to base their decisions on actual data, rather than personal observation. Internal auditors also may recommend controls for their organizations' computer systems to ensure the reliability of the systems and the integrity of the data.

Computers are rapidly changing the nature of the work for most accountants and auditors. With the aid of special software packages, accountants summarize transactions in standard formats for financial records and organize data in special formats for financial analysis. These accounting packages greatly reduce the amount of tedious manual work associated with data management and recordkeeping. Computers enable accountants and auditors to be more mobile and to use their clients' computer systems to extract information from databases and the Internet. As a result, a growing number of accountants and auditors with extensive computer skills specialize in correcting problems with software or in developing software to meet unique data management and analytical needs. Accountants also are beginning to perform more technical duties, such as implementing, controlling, and auditing systems and networks, and developing technology plans and budgets.

Increasingly, accountants also are assuming the role of a personal financial advisor. They not only provide clients with accounting and tax help, but also help them develop personal budgets, manage assets and investments, plan for retirement, and recognize and reduce exposure to risks. This role is a response to client demands for a single trustworthy individual or firm to meet all of their financial needs. However, accountants are restricted from providing these services to clients whose financial statements they also prepare. (See **financial analysts and personal financial advisors** elsewhere in the *Handbook*.)

Working Conditions

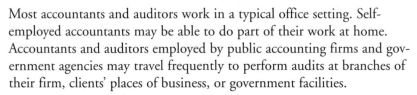

Questions Answered in This Section:

- What are the typical working hours for this job?
- What is the workplace environment for this job?
- What physical activities does this job require?
- How likely am I to be injured in this job?
- What special equipment would I need to know how to operate?
- How much travel does this job require?

Most accountants and auditors work in a typical office setting. Self-employed accountants may be able to do part of their work at home. Accountants and auditors employed by public accounting firms and government agencies may travel frequently to perform audits at branches of their firm, clients' places of business, or government facilities.

Most accountants and auditors generally work a standard 40-hour week, but many work longer hours, particularly if they are self-employed and have numerous clients. Tax specialists often work long hours during the tax season.

Employment

Questions Answered in This Section:

- How many jobs are there in this occupation?
- What industries are the jobs in?
- What percentage of workers in this job are self-employed?
- How many people in this job work part-time?
- In what geographic locations are the jobs?

Accountants and auditors held about 1.1 million jobs in 2002. They worked throughout private industry and government, but 1 out of 5 wage and salary accountants worked for accounting, tax preparation, bookkeeping, and payroll services firms. Approximately 1 out of 10 accountants or auditors were self-employed.

Many accountants and auditors are unlicensed management accountants, internal auditors, or government accountants and auditors; however, a large number are licensed Certified Public Accountants. Most accountants and auditors work in urban areas, where public accounting firms and central or regional offices of businesses are concentrated.

Some individuals with backgrounds in accounting and auditing are full-time college and university faculty; others teach part time while working as self-employed accountants or employed as accountants for private industry or government. (Elsewhere in the *Handbook* see **teachers—postsecondary**.)

Training, Other Qualifications, and Advancement

Questions Answered in This Section:

- What training and education do employers prefer for this job?
- How long will it take to train for this job?
- What are the possibilities for advancement on this job?
- What skills, aptitudes, and personal characteristics do I need in order to do this job?
- What certification and licensing does this job require?
- What opportunities for continuing education does this job provide?

Most accountant and auditor positions require at least a bachelor's degree in accounting or a related field. Beginning accounting and auditing positions in the federal government, for example, usually require 4 years of college (including 24 semester hours in accounting or auditing) or an equivalent combination of education and experience. Some employers prefer applicants with a master's degree in accounting, or with a master's degree in business administration with a concentration in accounting.

Previous experience in accounting or auditing can help an applicant get a job. Many colleges offer students an opportunity to gain experience through summer or part-time internship programs conducted by public accounting or business firms. In addition, practical knowledge of computers and their applications in accounting and internal auditing is a great asset for job seekers in the accounting field.

Professional recognition through certification or licensure provides a distinct advantage in the job market. CPAs are licensed by a State Board of Accountancy. The vast majority of states require CPA candidates to be college graduates, but a few states substitute a number of years of public accounting experience for a college degree. As of early 2003, based on recommendations made by the American Institute of Certified Public Accountants (AICPA), 42 states and the District of Columbia required CPA candidates to complete 150 semester hours of college coursework— an additional 30 hours beyond the usual 4-year bachelor's degree. Another five states—Arizona, Minnesota, New Mexico, New York, and Virginia— have adopted similar legislation that will become effective between 2004 and 2009. Colorado, Delaware, New Hampshire, and Vermont are the only states that do not require 150 semester hours. Many schools have altered their curricula accordingly, with most programs offering master's degrees as part of the 150 hours, and prospective accounting majors should carefully research accounting curricula and the requirements of any states in which they hope to become licensed.

All states use the four-part Uniform CPA Examination prepared by the AICPA. The 2-day CPA examination is rigorous, and only about one-quarter of those who take it each year passes every part they attempt. Candidates are not required to pass all four parts at once, but most states require candidates to pass at least two parts for partial credit and to complete all four sections within a certain period. Most states also require applicants for a CPA certificate to have some accounting experience. In May 2004, the CPA exam will become computerized and offered quarterly at various testing centers throughout the United States.

The AICPA also offers members with valid CPA certificates the option to receive the Accredited in Business Valuation (ABV), Certified Information Technology Professional (CITP), or Personal Financial Specialist (PFS) designations. The addition of these designations to the CPA distinguishes those accountants with a certain level of expertise in the nontraditional areas in which accountants are practicing more frequently. The ABV designation requires a written exam, as well as completion of a minimum of 10 business valuation projects that demonstrate a candidate's experience and competence. The CITP requires payment of a fee, a written statement of intent, and the achievement of a set number of points awarded for business experience and education. Those who do not meet the required number of points may substitute a written exam. Candidates for the PFS designation also must achieve a certain level of points, based on experience and education, and must pass a written exam and submit references.

Nearly all states require CPAs and other public accountants to complete a certain number of hours of continuing professional education before their licenses can be renewed. The professional associations representing accountants sponsor numerous courses, seminars, group study programs, and other forms of continuing education.

Accountants and auditors also can seek to obtain other forms of credentials from professional societies on a voluntary basis. Voluntary certification can attest to professional competence in a specialized field of accounting and auditing. It also can certify that a recognized level of professional competence has been achieved by accountants and auditors who have acquired some skills on the job, without the formal education or public accounting work experience needed to meet the rigorous standards required to take the CPA examination.

The Institute of Management Accountants (IMA) confers the Certified Management Accountant (CMA) designation upon applicants who complete a bachelor's degree or attain a minimum score on specified graduate school entrance exams. Applicants, who must have worked at least 2 years in management accounting, also must pass a four-part examination, agree to meet continuing education requirements, and comply with standards of professional conduct. The CMA program is administered by the Institute of Certified Management Accountants, an affiliate of the IMA.

Graduates from accredited colleges and universities who have worked for 2 years as internal auditors and have passed a four-part examination may earn the Certified Internal Auditor (CIA) designation from the Institute of Internal Auditors (IIA). The IIA recently implemented three new specialty designations—Certification in Control Self-Assessment (CCSA), Certified Government Auditing Professional (CGAP), and Certified Financial Services Auditor (CFSA). Requirements are similar to those of the CIA. The Information Systems Audit and Control Association confers the Certified Information Systems Auditor (CISA) designation upon candidates who pass an examination and have 5 years of experience in auditing information systems. Auditing or data-processing experience and a college education may be substituted for up to 2 years of work experience in this program. For instance, an internal auditor might be a CPA, CIA, and CISA.

The Accreditation Council for Accountancy and Taxation, a satellite organization of the National Society of Public Accountants, confers three designations—Accredited Business Accountant (ABA), Accredited Tax Advisor (ATA), and Accredited Tax Preparer (ATP)—on accountants specializing in tax preparation for small- and medium-sized businesses. Candidates for the ABA must pass an exam, while candidates for the ATA and ATP must complete the required coursework and pass an exam. Often, a practitioner will hold multiple licenses and designations.

The Association of Government Accountants grants the Certified Government Financial Manager (CGFM) designation for accountants, auditors, and other government financial personnel at the federal, state, and local levels. Candidates must have a minimum of a bachelor's degree, 24 hours of study in financial management, and 2 years' experience in government, and must pass a series of three exams. The exams cover topics in governmental environment; governmental accounting, financial reporting, and budgeting; and financial management and control.

Persons planning a career in accounting should have an <u>aptitude for mathematics</u> and be able to <u>analyze, compare,</u> and <u>interpret facts and figures</u> quickly. They must be able to <u>clearly communicate both in writing and verbally</u> the results of their work to clients and managers. Accountants and auditors must be <u>good at working with people,</u> as well as with <u>business systems and computers.</u> At a minimum, accountants should be <u>familiar with basic accounting software packages.</u> Because financial decisions are made based on their statements and services, accountants and auditors should have <u>high standards of integrity.</u>

Capable accountants and auditors may advance rapidly; those having inadequate academic preparation may be assigned routine jobs and find promotion difficult. Many graduates of junior colleges and business and correspondence schools, as well as bookkeepers and accounting clerks who meet the education and experience requirements set by their employers, can obtain junior accounting positions and advance to positions with more responsibilities by demonstrating their accounting skills on the job.

Beginning public accountants usually start by assisting with work for several clients. They may advance to positions with more responsibility in 1 or 2 years, and to senior positions within another few years. Those who excel may become supervisors, managers, or partners; open their own public accounting firm; or transfer to executive positions in management accounting or internal auditing in private firms.

Management accountants often start as cost accountants, junior internal auditors, or trainees for other accounting positions. As they rise through the organization, they may advance to accounting manager, chief cost accountant, budget director, or manager of internal auditing. Some become controllers, treasurers, financial vice presidents, chief financial officers, or corporation presidents. Many senior corporation executives have a background in accounting, internal auditing, or finance.

In general, public accountants, management accountants, and internal auditors have much occupational mobility. Practitioners often shift into management accounting or internal auditing from public accounting, or between internal auditing and management accounting. However, it is less common for accountants and auditors to move from either management accounting or internal auditing into public accounting.

Job Outlook

Questions Answered in This Section:
- Will there be more jobs available in this career in the future, or fewer?

- What factors are likely to influence the number of available jobs in this field?

Employment of accountants and auditors is expected to **grow about as fast as the average** for all occupations through the year 2012. An increase in the number of businesses, changing financial laws and regulations, and increased scrutiny of company finances will drive growth. In addition to openings resulting from growth, the need to replace accountants and auditors who retire or transfer to other occupations will produce numerous job openings in this large occupation.

As the economy grows, the number of business establishments will increase, requiring more accountants and auditors to set up books, prepare taxes, and provide management advice. As these businesses grow, the volume and complexity of information developed by accountants and auditors regarding costs, expenditures, and taxes will increase as well. Increased need for accountants and auditors will arise from changes in legislation related to taxes, financial reporting standards, business investments, mergers, and other financial matters. The growth of international business also has led to more demand for accounting expertise and services related to international trade and accounting rules, as well as to international mergers and acquisitions. These trends should create more jobs for accountants and auditors.

As a result of the recent accounting scandals, federal legislation was enacted to increase penalties and make company executives personally responsible for falsely reporting financial information. These changes should lead to increased scrutiny of company finances and accounting procedures, and should create opportunities for accountants and auditors, particularly Certified Public Accountants, to more thoroughly audit financial records. In order to ensure finances comply with the law before public accountants conduct audits, management accountants and internal auditors will increasingly be needed to discover and eliminate fraud. And, in an effort to make government agencies more efficient and accountable, demand for government accountants should increase.

Increased awareness of financial crimes such as embezzlement, bribery, and securities fraud will also increase the demand for forensic accountants to detect illegal financial activity by individuals, companies, and organized crime rings. Computer technology has made these crimes easier to commit, and they are on the rise. But development of new computer software and electronic surveillance technology has also made tracking down financial criminals easier, thus increasing the ease and likelihood that forensic accountants will discover their crimes. As success rates of investigations grow, demand will also grow for forensic accountants.

The changing role of accountants and auditors also will spur job growth, although this growth will be limited as a result of financial scandals. In response to demand, some accountants were offering more financial management and consulting services as they assumed a greater advisory role and developed more sophisticated accounting systems. Since federal legislation now prohibits accountants from providing nontraditional services to clients whose books they audit, opportunities for accountants to do non-audit work could be limited. However, accountants will still be able to advise on other financial matters for clients that are not publicly traded companies, and for nonaudit clients, but growth in these areas will be slower than in the past. Also, due to the increasing popularity of tax preparation firms and computer software, accountants will shift away from tax preparation. As computer programs continue to simplify some accounting-related tasks, clerical staff will increasingly handle many routine calculations.

Overall, job opportunities for accountants and auditors should be favorable. After most states instituted the 150-hour rule for CPAs, enrollment in accounting programs declined; however, enrollment is slowly beginning to grow again as more students are attracted to the profession because of the attention from the accounting scandals. Those who pursue a CPA should have excellent job prospects. However, many accounting graduates are instead pursuing other certifications such as the CMA and CIA, so competition could be greater in management accounting and internal auditing than in public accounting. Regardless of specialty, accountants and auditors who have earned professional recognition through certification or licensure should have the best job prospects. Applicants with a master's degree in accounting, or a master's degree in business administration with a concentration in accounting, also will have an advantage. In the aftermath of the accounting scandals, professional certification is even more important in order to ensure that accountants' credentials and ethics are sound.

Proficiency in accounting and auditing computer software, or expertise in specialized areas such as international business, specific industries, or current legislation, may be helpful in landing certain accounting and auditing jobs. In addition, employers increasingly seek applicants with strong interpersonal and communication skills. Because many accountants work on teams with others from different backgrounds, they must be able to communicate accounting and financial information clearly and concisely. Regardless of one's qualifications, however, competition will remain keen for the most prestigious jobs in major accounting and business firms.

Earnings

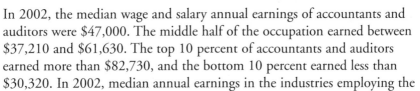

Questions Answered in This Section:

- How much money am I likely to make in this job?

- How will I be paid in this job—salaried, hourly, commissions, tips, piece rates, or bonuses?

- What other benefits might this job include?

In 2002, the median wage and salary annual earnings of accountants and auditors were $47,000. The middle half of the occupation earned between $37,210 and $61,630. The top 10 percent of accountants and auditors earned more than $82,730, and the bottom 10 percent earned less than $30,320. In 2002, median annual earnings in the industries employing the largest numbers of accountants and auditors were:

Federal Government	$51,070
Accounting, tax preparation, bookkeeping, and payroll services	49,520
Management of companies and enterprises	49,110
Local government	44,690
State government	42,680

According to a salary survey conducted by the National Association of Colleges and Employers, bachelor's degree candidates in accounting received starting offers averaging $40,647 a year in 2003; master's degree candidates in accounting were initially offered $42,241.

According to a 2003 salary survey conducted by Robert Half International, a staffing services firm specializing in accounting and finance, accountants and auditors with up to 1 year of experience earned between $29,500 and $40,500. Those with 1 to 3 years of experience earned between $34,000 and $49,500. Senior accountants and auditors earned between $41,000 and $61,500; managers earned between $47,500 and $78,750; and directors of accounting and auditing earned between $66,750 and $197,500 a year. The variation in salaries reflects differences in size of firm, location, level of education, and professional credentials.

In the federal government, the starting annual salary for junior accountants and auditors was $23,442 in 2003. Candidates who had a superior academic record might start at $29,037, while applicants with a master's degree or 2 years of professional experience usually began at $35,519. Beginning salaries were slightly higher in selected areas where the prevailing local pay level was higher. Accountants employed by the federal government in nonsupervisory, supervisory, and managerial positions averaged $69,370 a year in 2003; auditors averaged $73,247.

Related Occupations

Questions Answered in This Section:
- What other jobs involve similar duties?
- What other jobs require similar skills, education, and training?

Accountants and auditors design internal control systems and analyze financial data. Others for whom training in accounting is valuable include budget analysts; cost estimators; loan officers; financial analysts and personal financial advisors; tax examiners, collectors, and revenue agents; bill and account collectors; and bookkeeping, accounting, and auditing clerks. Recently, accountants have assumed the role of management analysts and are involved in the design, implementation, and maintenance of accounting software systems. Others who perform similar work include computer programmers, computer software engineers, and computer support specialists and systems administrators.

Sources of Additional Information

Questions Answered in This Section:
- Where can I learn more about this job on the Internet?
- What are some of the professional associations for people employed in this job?

Disclaimer:

Links to non-BLS Internet sites are provided for your convenience and do not constitute an endorsement.

Information on accredited accounting programs can be obtained from:

- AACSB International—Association to Advance Collegiate Schools of Business, 600 Emerson Rd., Suite 300, St. Louis, MO 63141. Internet:
  http://www.aacsb.edu/accreditation/AccreditedMembers.asp

Information about careers in certified public accounting and CPA standards and examinations may be obtained from:

- American Institute of Certified Public Accountants, 1211 Avenue of the Americas, New York, NY 10036. Internet: **http://www.aicpa.org**

Information on CPA licensure requirements by state may be obtained from:

- National Association of State Boards of Accountancy, 150 Fourth Ave. North, Suite 700, Nashville, TN 37219-2417. Internet: **http://www.nasba.org**

Information on careers in management accounting and the CMA designation may be obtained from:

- Institute of Management Accountants, 10 Paragon Dr., Montvale, NJ 07645-1760. Internet: **http://www.imanet.org**

Information on the Accredited in Accountancy, Accredited Business Accountant, Accredited Tax Advisor, or Accredited Tax Preparer designations may be obtained from:

- Accreditation Council for Accountancy and Taxation, 1010 North Fairfax St., Alexandria, VA 22314. Internet: **http://www.acatcredentials.org**

Information on careers in internal auditing and the CIA designation may be obtained from:

- The Institute of Internal Auditors, 247 Maitland Ave., Altamonte Springs, FL 32701-4201. Internet: **http://www.theiia.org**

Information on careers in information systems auditing and the CISA designation may be obtained from:

- Information Systems Audit and Control Association, 3701 Algonquin Rd., Suite 1010, Rolling Meadows, IL 60008. Internet: **http://www.isaca.org**

Information on careers in government accounting and the CGFM designation may be obtained from:

- Association of Government Accountants, 2208 Mount Vernon Ave., Alexandria, VA 22301. Internet: **http://www.agacgfm.org**

Information on obtaining an accounting or auditing position with the federal government is available from the U.S. Office of Personnel Management (OPM) through a telephone-based system. Consult your telephone directory under U.S. Government for a local number or call (703) 724-1850; Federal Relay Service: (800) 877-8339. The first number is not toll free, and charges may result. Information also is available from the OPM Internet site: **http://www.usajobs.opm.gov**.

A Short List of Additional Resources

Thousands of books and uncounted Internet sites provide information on career subjects. Space limitations do not permit me to describe the many good resources available, so I list here some of the most useful ones. Because this is my list, I've included books I've written or that JIST publishes. You should be able to find these and many other resources at libraries, bookstores, and Web bookselling sites such as Amazon.com.

Resume and Cover Letter Books

My Books

- Now in its third edition, *The Quick Resume & Cover Letter Book* is one of the top-selling resume books at various large bookstore chains. It is very simple to follow, is inexpensive, has good design, and has good sample resumes written by professional resume writers.

- *Same-Day Resume* is a quick book in the *Help in a Hurry* series, as is this book. In it you will find advice that will help you do a simple resume in an hour and a better one later.

- *15-Minute Cover Letter,* co-authored with Louise Kursmark, is another book in the *Help in a Hurry* series. It contains a gallery of sample cover letters and tips for writing them fast and effectively.

Other Books Published by JIST

The following titles include many sample resumes written by professional resume writers, as well as good advice:

- *Amazing Resumes,* Jim Bright, Ph.D., and Joanne Earl, Ph.D.

- *Cover Letter Magic,* Wendy S. Enelow and Louise M. Kursmark

- *Expert Resumes for Career Changers,* Enelow and Kursmark

- *Expert Resumes for Computer and Web Jobs,* Enelow and Kursmark
- *Expert Resumes for Health Care Careers,* Enelow and Kursmark
- *Expert Resumes for Managers and Executives,* Enelow and Kursmark
- *Expert Resumes for Military-to-Civilian Transitions,* Enelow and Kursmark
- *Expert Resumes for People Returning to Work,* Enelow and Kursmark
- *Expert Resumes for Teachers and Educators,* Enelow and Kursmark
- *Federal Resume Guidebook,* Kathryn Kraemer Troutman
- *Gallery of Best Resumes, Gallery of Best Cover Letters,* and *Gallery of Best Resumes for People Without a Four-Year Degree,* David F. Noble
- *Résumé Magic,* Susan Britton Whitcomb

Job Search Books

My Books

- *The Very Quick Job Search* is a thorough book with detailed advice and a "quick" section of key tips you can finish in a few hours.
- *Getting the Job You Really Want* includes many in-the-book activities and good career decision-making and job search advice.

Other Books Published by JIST

- *Inside Secrets to Finding a Teaching Job,* Jack Warner, Clyde Bryan, and Diane Warner
- *Insider's Guide to Finding a Job,* Wendy S. Enelow and Shelly Goldman
- *Job Search Handbook for People with Disabilities,* Dr. Daniel J. Ryan
- *Job Search Magic,* Susan Britton Whitcomb
- *Over-40 Job Search Guide,* Gail Geary
- *Ultimate Job Search,* Richard H. Beatty

Books About Interviewing for Jobs

- *Next-Day Job Interview,* in which I give quick tips for preparing for a job interview at the last minute

- *Interview Magic,* in which Susan Britton Whitcomb coaches readers through the interview process

Books with Information on Jobs

Primary References

All of these books are available from JIST.

- The *Occupational Outlook Handbook* is the source of job titles listed in this book. Published by the U.S. Department of Labor and updated every other year, the *OOH* covers about 87 percent of the workforce.

- A book titled the *O*NET Dictionary of Occupational Titles* has descriptions for more than 1,000 jobs based on the O*NET (for Occupational Information Network) database developed by the Department of Labor.

- The *Enhanced Occupational Outlook Handbook* includes the *OOH* descriptions plus more than 2,000 additional descriptions of related jobs from the O*NET and other sources.

- The *New Guide for Occupational Exploration* allows you to explore major jobs based on your interests.

Other Books Published by JIST

Here are a few good books that include job descriptions and helpful details on career options:

- **These books include selected jobs from the *OOH* and other information:** *100 Fastest-Growing Careers, Top 100 Careers for College Graduates, Top 100 Careers for People Without a Four-Year Degree,* and *Top 100 Computer and Technical Careers*

- **Books in the *Best Jobs* series, including the following:** *Best Jobs for the 21st Century, 200 Best Jobs for College Graduates, 250 Best Jobs Through Apprenticeships, 300 Best Jobs Without a Four-Year Degree,* and *50 Best Jobs for Your Personality*

- *Overnight Career Choice,* a quick guide to discovering your ideal job in just a few hours

Internet Resources

There are too many Web sites to list, but here are a few places you can start.

- A book by Anne Wolfinger titled **Best Career and Education Web Sites** gives unbiased reviews of the most helpful sites and ideas on how to use them. The *Occupational Outlook Handbook*'s job descriptions also include Internet addresses for related organizations. And www.jist.com lists recommended sites for career, education, and related topics, along with comments on each.

- *Job Seeker's Online Goldmine,* by Janet Wall, is your guide to the extensive free online job search tools from government and other sources

Be aware that some sites provide poor advice, so ask your librarian, instructor, or counselor for suggestions on those best for your needs.

Other Resources

Libraries

Most libraries have the books mentioned here, as well as many other resources. Many also provide Internet access so that you can research online information. Ask the librarian for help finding what you need.

People

People who hold the jobs that interest you are one of the best career information sources. Ask them what they like and don't like about their work, how they got started, and the education or training needed. Most people are helpful and will give advice you can't get any other way.

Career Counseling

A good vocational counselor can help you explore career options. Take advantage of this service if it is available to you! Also consider a career-planning course or program, which will encourage you to be more thorough in your thinking.

Index

A

accepting job offers, 136–137
accomplishments, 64, 77–78, 145–146
accountants, 19, 156–170
action words, 64, 76–77
actors, 22
actuaries, 19
adaptive skills. *See* personality traits; self-
  management skills
addresses
  e-mail, 71–72
  mailing, 71
  cover letters, 95
  interviewers, 122
administrative services managers, 18
adult literacy teachers, 22
advertisements, 37
  Internet, 38–39
  job openings, 47
  job searches, 62
  small business, 65
advertising and public relations services,
  18, 32
aerospace engineers, 20
aerospace product and parts manufacturing, 31
agricultural engineers, 20
agricultural scientists, 21
agricultural workers, 27
agriculture, forestry, and fishing, 31
agriculture, mining, and construction, 31
air traffic controllers, 30
air transportation occupations, 30–31
aircraft and avionics equipment mechanics
  and service technicians, 28
aircraft pilots and flight engineers, 30
alignment of text in resumes, 93
Amazing Resumes, 171
animal care and service workers, 2
announcers, 22
apparel manufacturing, 31
appearance, 117, 120–121
applications for jobs, 37, 39, 50
appraisers, 19
architects, surveyors, and cartographers, 20
archivists, 22

armed forces, 30, 76, 82–83
art and design occupations, 22
artistic skills, 11
artists, 22
assemblers and fabricators, 29
assessments
  job objectives, 13–16
  skills, 3, 5–12, 155
astronomers, 21
athletes, 22
atmospheric scientists, 21
audiologists, 23
auditors, 19, 156–170
automobile dealers, 31
automotive body and related repairers, 28
automotive service technicians and mechanics, 28
availability for jobs, JIST Cards, 52–53
awards and recognition, 78

B

banking, 32
barbers, cosmetologists, and personal
  appearance workers, 25
Beatty, Richard H., 172
benefits, 16, 156
Best Career and Education Web Sites, 174
Best Jobs for the 21st Century, 173
bill and account collectors, 26
billing and posting clerks and machine
  operators, 26
biological scientists, 21
biomedical engineers, 20
blind mailing, 42
body language, 121
boilermakers, 27
bold fonts, 92, 94
bookbinders and bindery workers, 29
bookkeeping, accounting, and auditing
  clerks, 26
brackets, salary, 134–135
brickmasons, blockmasons,
  and stonemasons, 27
Bright, Jim, 171
broadcasting, 22, 32
brokerage clerks, 26
Bryan, Clyde, 172

budget analysts, 19
building and grounds cleaning and
maintenance, 24–25
bulleted lists, 92
bus drivers, 30
business occupations, 18–19
buyers, 19

C

call-back close, 127
cardiovascular technologists and technicians, 23
career centers at universities, 41
career counseling, 4, 174
Career Guide to Industries, 30
cargo and freight agents, 26
carpenters, 27
carpet, floor, and tile installers and
finishers, 27
cartographers, 20
cashiers, 25
cement masons, concrete finishers, segmental pavers, and terrazzo workers, 27
certifications, listing on resumes, 92, 101
Certified Public Accountants (CPAs), 157
checklists. *See* worksheets
chefs, cooks, and food preparation
workers, 24
chemical engineers, 20
chemical manufacturing, 31
chemists, 21, 54
childcare workers, 25, 32
chiropractors, 23
chitchat during interviews, 122
choreographers, 22
chronological resumes, 66, 68
   awards and recognition, 78
   e-mail addresses, 71–72
   education and training, 75–76
   final draft, 79–80
   job objectives, 72–75
   mailing addresses, 71
   name, 71
   personal information, 78–79
   phone numbers, 71–72
   professional organizations, 78
   references, 79
   simple and improved examples, 69–70
   volunteer experience, 76
   work experience, 76–78
civil engineers, 20
claims adjusters, 19

clarity in cover letters, 95
classmates, networking, 44
clergy, 21
clinical laboratory technologists and technicians, 23
closing interviews, 125, 127
clothing, accessory, and general merchandise stores, 31
co-workers, 14, 43
coaches, 22
coin, vending, and amusement machine servicers and repairers, 28
cold contacts, 42, 46–49, 57, 65, 142
combination resumes, 67
communication skills, 4, 10, 122–123
communications equipment operators, 25
community association managers, 19
community services, 21
competitive work environment, 124
compliments during interviews, 122
computer and electronic product
manufacturing, 31
computer occupations, 18–20, 25, 29, 32,
54, 100
computer, automated teller, and office
machine repairers, 28
conservation scientists, 21
construction management, 102
construction trades, 18, 27–28, 31
contact information, 51, 71–72
contacts
   contacting employers, 46–49, 59, 119
   daily job search contact sheets, 142–143
   networking, 43–46
control statements, 123
corporate accountants, 158
correctional officers, 24
correctional treatment specialists, 21
correspondents, 22
cost accountants, 158
cost estimators, 19
counseling careers, 21, 174
counter and rental clerks, 25
couriers and messengers, 26
court reporters, 21
Cover Letter Magic, 171
cover letters, 94–99, 171–172
creative skills, 11
credit authorizers, checkers, and clerks, 26
curators, 22
curriculum vitae (CV), 66–68
customer service representatives, 25

D

daily job search contact sheets, 142–143
dancers, 22
data analysis skills, 10
data entry and information processing
  workers, 25
database administrators, 20
databases of resumes, 59
demonstrators, product promoters, and
  models, 25
dental assistants, 24
dental hygienists, 23
dental laboratory technicians, 29
dentists, 23
Department of Labor, 39–40
designing resumes, 64, 92–93
designers, 22
desktop publishers, 26
development management, 102
diagnostic medical sonographers, 23
diesel service technicians and mechanics, 28
dietitians, 23
directors, 22
disabilities, people with, 172
dispatchers, 26
diversity in the workplace, 61–62
drafters and engineering technicians, 20
dressing for interviews, 117, 120–121
drywall installers, ceiling tile installers, and
  tapers, 27
duties and accomplishments, 77–78

E

e-mail
  addresses on resumes, 71–72
  contacting interviewers, 65, 119
  sending JIST Cards, 50
  sending resumes, 42, 65
Earl, Joanne, 171
earnings. See salary
economists, 21
editors, 23
education administrators, 19
education and health services, 32
education and training, 146–147
  chronological resumes, 75–76
  examples, 69–70, 101–108
  JIST Cards, 52
  Occupational Outlook Handbook
    (OOH), 161–164
education, training, library, and museum
  occupations, 22

educational services, 32
electrical and electronic equipment
  mechanics, installers, and repairers, 28
electrical and electronics engineers, 20
electricians, 27
electronic home entertainment equipment
  installers and repairers, 28
electronic resumes, 59, 92–94
electronic schedulers, 115
electronics installation, 55
elementary teachers, 22
elevator installers and repairers, 27
emergency medical technicians and
  paramedics, 23
employers. See also interviews
  cold contacts, 42, 46–49, 59
  effective resume uses, 65–66
  fee-based agencies, 40
  filling out applications, 39
  most-desired skills, 4
  previous, 77
employment agencies, 39–41
employment dates, 77
employment outlook, 160–161
employment services, 32
Enelow, Wendy S., 17, 68, 172
engineering and natural sciences
  managers, 19
engineering technicians, 20
engineers, 20
entertainers and performers, sports
  occupations, 22
entry-level jobs, 39
environment at work, 15, 124, 160
environmental engineers, 20
environmental scientists, 21
examiners, 19
executive management styles, 124
executives, 19
Expert Resumes for Career Changers, 171
Expert Resumes for Computer and Web Jobs,
  172
Expert Resumes for Health Care Careers, 172
Expert Resumes for Managers and Executives,
  172
Expert Resumes for Military-to-Civilian
  Transitions, 172
Expert Resumes for People Returning to Work,
  172
Expert Resumes for Teachers and Educators,
  68, 172
extracurricular activities, 146–147
eye contact during interviews, 121

F

farmers, ranchers, and agricultural managers, 19

farming, fishing, and forestry occupations, 27

federal government, 32

Federal Resume Guidebook, 172

fees for employment agencies, 40

15-Minute Cover Letter, 171

50 Best Jobs for Your Personality, 173

file clerks, 26

financial activities, 32

financial analysts, 19

financial clerks, 26

financial operations, 18–19

firefighting occupations, 24

first impressions during interviews, 117–122

fishers and fishing vessel operators, 27

flight attendants, 25

following up
  cover letters, 95
  after interviews, 127–128
  with JIST Cards, 65
  organizing system for, 140–143
  with thank-you notes, 65, 139–140

fonts, 92–94

food and beverage serving, 24

food manufacturing, 31

food preparation and serving occupations, 24

food processing occupations, 29

food scientists, 21

food service managers, 19

forensic accounting, 158

forest, conservation, and logging workers, 27

foresters, 21

formats. *See* cover letters; resumes

40 Best Fields for Your Career, 30

friends, networking, 43

functional resumes. *See* skills resumes

funeral directors, 19

G

Gallery of Best Cover Letters, 172

Gallery of Best Resumes, 172

Gallery of Best Resumes for People Without a Four-Year Degree, 172

gaming cage workers, 26

gaming services occupations, 25

Geary, Gail, 172

general office/clerical, 53

geoscientists, 21

Getting the Job You Really Want, 172

glaziers, 27

goals of employers, 125

Goldman, Shelly, 172

goods-producing industries, 31

government accountants and auditors, 158

government employment agencies, 39–40

government industries, 32

graphics on resumes, 67, 92–94

grocery stores, 31

grooming for interviews, 117, 120–121

grounds maintenance workers, 25

H

handshakes at interviews, 121

hazardous materials removal workers, 27

health diagnosing and treating practitioners, 23

health services, 32

health technologists and technicians, 23–24

healthcare support occupations, 24

heating, air-conditioning, and refrigeration mechanics and installers, 28

heavy vehicle and mobile equipment service technicians and mechanics, 28

Help in a Hurry series, 171

hobbies, 146–147

home appliance repairers, 28

honesty on resumes, 64

hotel management, 56

hotel, motel, and resort desk clerks, 26

human resources assistants, except payroll and timekeeping, 26

human resources, training, and labor relations managers, 19

human service assistants, 21

I

industrial accountants, 158

industrial engineers, 20

industrial machinery installation, repair, and maintenance workers, 28

industrial production managers, 19

industries, 31–32

information and record clerks, 26

information industries, 32

information systems managers, 18

Inside Secrets to Finding a Teaching Job, 172

Insider's Guide to Finding a Job, 172

inspectors, testers, sorters, samplers, and weighers, 29

installation, maintenance, and repair occupations, 28
instructional coordinators, 22
insulation workers, 27
insurance, 32
insurance sales agents, 25
insurance underwriters, 19
internal auditors, 159
international jobs, 62
Internet. *See also* Web sites
  books, 174
  electronic resumes, creating, 90–94
  help-wanted ads, 38–39
  job searches, 58–60
  posting resumes, 41–42, 59, 65–66
interpersonal skills, 4
interpreters, 22
Interview Magic, 173
interviewers, 26, 119, 122
interviews
  answering questions, 124–126, 128–131
  asking questions, 124–125
  closing, 126–127
  communicating skills, 122–123
  contacting employers, 65
  control statements, 123
  first impressions, 117–122
  following up, 65, 127–128, 139–140
  presenting weaknesses, 5
  salary negotiations, 131–137
  scheduling, 111
investigators, 19
italic font, 92

J

jewelers and precious stone and metal workers, 29
JIST books, 171–174
JIST Cards, 49–57, 144
  following up, 65, 139
  networking, 65
job lead cards, 140–141
job objectives
  chronological resumes, 72–75
  defining ideal job, 13–17
  education related to, 146
  exploring jobs and industries, 17–33
  in Internet searches, 58
  on JIST Cards, 51
  job-related skills requirements, 34–35
  self-employment, 33–34
  skills resumes, 87
job offers, 135–137

job openings, 47–49
job outlooks, 165–167
job requirements, 34–35
Job Search Handbook for People with Disabilities, 172
Job Search Magic, 172
job searches
  applications, 39
  books, 171–174
  contacting employers directly, 46–49
  employment agencies, 39–41
  help-wanted ads, 38–39
  Internet, 41–42, 58–62
  JIST Cards, 49–57
  mailing/posting resumes, 41–42
  methods most used, 37–38
  networking, 43–46
  scheduling, 112–115
  special employment services, 41
  using OOH descriptions, 155–156
Job Seeker's Online Goldmine, 174
job targets, 155
job-related skills, 5, 12, 34–35, 52
judges, 22
judicial workers, 22

K–L

key skills, 74, 88–92
keywords, 59
kindergarten teachers, 22
knowledge areas, 14
Kursmark, Louise M., 68, 172
landscape architects, 20
lawyers, 22
leadership skills, 4, 10
leads, networking, 45, 144
legal occupations, 21–22
leisure activities, 146–147
length of resumes, 64
length of unemployment, 112
length of interviews, 125
librarians, 22
libraries, 174
library assistants, clerical, 26
library technicians, 22
licensed practical and licensed vocational nurses, 23
licenses, listing on electronic resumes, 92
life scientists, 21
line installers and repairers, 28
loan counselors/officers, 19
location of workplace, 15
lodging managers, 19

M

machine setters, operators, and tenders—metal and plastic, 29
machinists, 29
magistrates, 22
mailing addresses, 71
mailing resumes, 41–42
maintenance and repair workers, 28
management accountants, 158
management occupations, 18–19
management styles, 124
management, hotels, 56
management, scientific, and technical consulting services, 32
management, warehouse, 55
managerial accountants, 158
manufacturing, 31
margins on electronic resumes, 94
market researchers, 21
marketing, 18
material moving occupations, 30
material-recording, -scheduling, -dispatching, and -distributing occupations, 26
materials engineers, 20
materials scientists, 21
mathematical occupations, 19–20
mechanical engineers, 20
media and communications occupations, 22
medical and health services, 19
medical assistants, 24
medical records and health information technicians, 23
medical scientists, 21
medical transcriptionists, 24
metal workers and plastic workers, 29
meter readers, utilities, 26
middle-school teachers, 22
military experience, 76, 82–83
millwrights, 28
mining, 31
mining and geological engineers, 20
ministers, 21
motion picture and video industries, 32
motor vehicle and parts manufacturing, 31
museum technicians, 22
musicians, 22

N

names on resumes, 71, 122
nature of the work, 156–159
negotiating benefits and salaries, 131–136, 156

neighbors, networking, 43
networking, 43–46
    via Internet, 59–60
    JIST Cards, 50, 65
    people with similar jobs, 174
    referrals, 142
news analysts, 22
newspaper advertisements, 38–39
Next-Day Job Interview, 173
Noble, David F., 172
nuclear engineers, 20
nuclear medicine technologists, 24
nursing, psychiatric, and home health aides, 24
nutritionists, 23

O

O*NET Dictionary of Occupational Titles, 92, 156
objectives. See job objectives
occupational health and safety specialists and technicians, 24
Occupational Outlook Handbook (OOH), 92, 173
    earnings, 167–168
    employment, 160–161
    job outlook, 165–167
    nature of the work, 156–159
    related occupations, 168–169
    significant points, 156
    sources of additional information, 169–170
    training, other qualifications, and advancement, 161–164
    using in job search, 155–156
    working conditions, 160
occupational therapist assistants and aides, 24
occupational therapists, 23
office and administrative support, 25–27
office clerks, general, 27
oil and gas extraction, 31
100 Fastest-Growing Careers, 173
One-Stop government employment agencies, 40
online searches. See Internet; Web sites
operations research analysts, 20
ophthalmic laboratory technicians, 29
opticians, dispensing, 24
optometrists, 23
order clerks, 26
organization skills, 4

Over-40 Job Search Guide, 172
Overnight Career Choice, 174

P

painters and paperhangers, 27
painting and coating workers, 29
paper
  cover letters, 95
  JIST Cards, 53
  resumes, 67
paper resumes into electronic resumes, 94
paragraph indents, 93
paralegals, 22
payroll and timekeeping clerks, 26
people skills, 4, 10, 122–123
personality traits, 4, 6–8, 53
personal and home care aides, 25
personal care and service occupations, 25
personal digital assistants (PDAs), 115, 143
personal financial advisors, 19
personal information, 51, 69, 78–79, 86, 145
personality traits, 4–6, 14, 53, 124, 126
pest control workers, 25
petroleum engineers, 20
pharmaceutical and medicine manufacturing, 31
pharmacists, 23
pharmacy aides/technicians, 24
photogrammetrists, 20
photographers, 22
photographic process workers and processing machine operators, 29
physical scientists, 21
physical therapist assistants and aides, 23–24
physician assistants, 23
physicians and surgeons, 23
physicists, 21
pipelayers, plumbers, pipefitters, and steamfitters, 27
plant and system operators, 29
plasterers and stucco masons, 28
podiatrists, 23
police and detectives, 24
postal service workers, 27
posting resumes online, 91
postsecondary teachers, 22
power plant operators, distributors, and dispatchers, 29
precision instrument and equipment repairers, 28
prepress technicians and workers, 29

preschool teachers, 22
priests, 21
printing machine operators, 29
printing occupations, 29, 31
private accountants, 158
private detectives and investigators, 24
private employment agencies, 37, 40
probational officers, 21
problem questions during interviews, 124
problem-solving skills, 4
procurement clerks, 26
producers, 22
production occupations, 29–30
production, planning, and expediting clerks, 26
professional and business services, 32
professional occupations, 19–24
professional organizations, 44
  chronological resumes, 78, 86
  networking, 60
  resumes, 101, 105
project manager, 103
promotions, 18
proofreading resumes, 64
property managers, 19
protective service occupations, 24
Prove-It Technique, 129–130
psychologists, 21
public accountants, 157–158
public relations, 18, 23
publishing, 32
punctuality for interviews, 118, 120
purchasing agents, 19
purchasing managers, 19

Q

questions
  control statements, 123
  answering in interviews, 124–126, 128–131
  asking in interviews, 122–125
  networking, 45
The Quick Resume & Cover Letter Book, 171

R

rabbis, 21
radio and telecommunications equipment installers and repairers, 28
radio operators, 22
radiologic technologists and technicians, 24
rail transportation occupations, 30
ranges for salaries, 133–134
real estate occupations, 19, 25

receptionists and information clerks, 26
receptionists with potential employers, 118
recognition and awards, 78
recreation and fitness workers, 25
recreational therapists, 23
references, 79, 153–154
referrals, 45, 65, 97, 142, 144
regional planners, 21
registered nurses, 23
rejecting job offers, 135–136
related occupations, 168–169
related skills, 130
relatives, networking, 43
religious groups, networking, 43
relocation, 15, 59
remedial teachers, 22
reporters, 22
rescheduling interviews, 121
researching
    employers, 118
    industries, 33
    job titles, 33
    salaries, 132
reservation and transportation ticket agents
    and travel clerks, 26
responsibilities on the job, 16, 73
Résumé Magic, 172
resumes
    action words, 76
    books, 171–172
    chronological resumes, 66, 68–80
    combination resumes, 67
    curriculum vitae (CV), 67–68
    e-mailing, 42, 65
    effective uses, 65–66
    electronic resumes, 41–42, 59, 90–94
    examples, 69–70, 93, 99–108
    graphics, 67
    JIST Cards, 49–57
    mailing, 41–42
    scannable resumes, 90–94
    skills resumes, 66–67, 87–90
    tips for creating, 63–65
    updating, 156
retail salespersons, 25
roofers, 28
Ryan, Dr. Daniel J., 172

S

salary
    negotiation, 131–136
    Occupational Outlook Handbook
        (OOH), 167–168
    requirements, 15–16, 18, 124, 132, 156

sales engineers, 25
sales managers, 18
sales occupations, 25
sales representatives, wholesale and
    manufacturing, 25
sales worker supervisors, 25
Same-Day Resume, 171
scannable resumes, 90–94
scheduling
    electronic schedulers, 115
    interviews, 111, 120
    follow-ups, 127–128
    job searches, 114
schools, 41
science technicians, 21
screening process, 132, 135
secondary teachers, 22
secretaries and administrative assistants, 27
securities, commodities, and other invest-
    ments, 25, 32
security guards and gaming surveillance
    officers, 24
self-employment, 33–34
self-enrichment education teachers, 22
self-management skills, 4, 6–8
semiconductor processors, 29
service occupations, 24–25
service-producing industries, 31–32
sheet metal workers, 28
shipping, receiving, and traffic clerks, 26
singers, 22
skills
    emphasizing in interviews, 155
    employer's wishlist, 4
    ideal-job requirements, 34–35
    identifying, 5–12
    job-related, 5, 12, 52
    personality traits, 4, 6–8, 53
    related, presenting in interviews, 130
    in skills resumes, 87–88
    soft, 5
    transferable, 4, 8–11
skills resumes, 66–67, 87–90
small businesses, 49, 65
small engine mechanics, 28
small talk during interviews, 122
smoking during interviews, 120
social assistance occupations, 32
social clubs, 44
social scientists, 21
social services, 21
soft skills, 5
software publishers, 32
sound engineering technicians, 22

special education teachers, 22
speech-language pathologists, 23
state and local government, 32
stationary engineers and boiler
   operators, 29
statisticians, 20
steel manufacturing, 31
stock clerks and order fillers, 27
strengths and weaknesses, 5, 67, 70, 124,
   126
structural and reinforcing iron and metal
   workers, 28
surgical technologists, 24
survey researchers, 21
surveying technicians, 20
surveyors, 20
systems administrators, 20
systems analysts, 54

T

tab indents on resumes, 93
tables on resumes, 93
target audience, cover letters, 94
tax examiners, collectors, and revenue
   agents, 19
taxi drivers and chauffeurs, 30
teacher assistants, 22
teachers, 22, 44
telecommunications, 32
telephones
   phone numbers, 71–72
   phone scripts, 57
   phone interviews, 119
   yellow pages, 46–47
television, video, and motion picture
   camera operators, and editors, 23
tellers, 26
temporary agencies, 40–41
text alignment on resumes, 93
textile mills and products, 31
textile, apparel, and furnishings occupations, 29
thank-you notes, 50, 65, 127, 139–140
300 Best Jobs Without a Four-Year Degree,
   173
Three-Step Process, interview questions,
   128–130
tool and die makers, 29
Top 100 Careers for College Graduates, 173
*Top 100 Careers for People Without a
   Four-Year Degree,* 173
Top 100 Computer and Technical Careers,
   173

top executives, 19
trade industries, 31
training. *See* education and training
transferable skills, 4, 8–11, 88–90
translators, 22
transportation and material moving occupations, 30
transportation and utilities, 31–32
travel agents, 25
travel requirements for jobs, 160
Troutman, Kathryn Kraemer, 172
truck drivers and driver/sales workers, 30
truck transportation and warehousing, 31
200 Best Jobs for College Graduates, 173
250 Best Jobs Through Apprenticeships, 173

U–V

Ultimate Job Search, 172
umpires, 22
unemployment
   government agencies, 39–40
   length, 112
   surveys, 37–38
updating resumes, 156
urban planners, 21
utilities occupations, 32
values, job objectives, 16
vehicle and mobile equipment mechanics,
   installers, and repairers, 28
The Very Quick Job Search, 172
veterinarians, 23
veterinary technologists and technicians, 24
voice during interviews, 121–122
voice-mail messages, 72
volunteer experience, 76, 86, 148–153

W–Z

walk-ins for interviews, 48
Wall, Janet, 174
warehouse management, 55
warm contacts
   JIST Cards, 57
   networking, 42–46
Warner, Diane and Jack, 172
water and liquid waste treatment plant and
   system operators, 29
water transportation occupations, 30
weaknesses, presenting, 5, 124, 126
Web sites
   *Accreditation Council for Accountancy
      and Taxation, 170*
   America Online, 60
   America's Career Information Network, 60

America's Job Bank, 40, 61
American Institute of Certified Public
    Accountants, 169
Association of Government Accountants,
    170
Association to Advance Collegiate Schools
    of Business (AACSB International), 169
Bureau of Labor Statistics, 30
Career Masters Institute, 99
CareerBank, 61
CareerBuilder, 38, 60–61
CareerJournal, 61
CareerOINK, 30, 60
CollegeGrad.com, 61
dice.com, 61
diversity recruiting, 61–62
Employment and Training Admin-
    istration, 40
eRecruiting, 61
Executives on the Web, 61
Google, 72
Hire Diversity, 62
Hotmail, 72
IMDiversity, 62
Information Systems Audit and Control
    Association, 170
Institute of Internal Auditors, 170
Institute of Management Accountants, 170
international jobs, 62
JIST, 50, 60
Job Central, 61
Job Street, 62
JobsDB, 62
Jobsinthemoney, 61
LatPro, 61
Microsoft Network, 60
Monster.com, 39, 61
National Association of Colleges and
    Employers, 61
National Association of State Boards of
    Accountancy, 169
National Résumé Writers' Association, 99
networking, 59
Occupational Outlook Handbook
    (OOH), 18
Professional Association of Résumé Writers
    and Career Coaches, 99
Riley Guide, 60
Service Locator, 40
6FigureJobs, 61
Small Business Administration, 33
Workopolis, 62

Yahoo! HotJobs, 61, 72
yellow pages, 48
weighers, measurers, checkers, and samplers,
    recordkeeping, 27
welding, soldering, and brazing workers, 29
Whitcomb, Susan Britton, 172
wholesale trade, 31
Wolfinger, Anne, 174
woodworkers, 29
work conditions/environment, 15, 124, 160
work experience, 148–153
    combination resumes, 100–108
    chronological resumes, 66, 76–78
    JIST Cards, 51–52
Workforce Development, 39–40
working arrangements, JIST Cards, 52–53
workplaces, location of, 15
worksheets
    choosing ideal job, 14–16
    Describe Your Current Job Objective in
        General Terms, 13
    Essential Job Search Data, 145–154
    Identify Your Key Transferable Skills, 89
    Instant Resume, 80–86
    The Job Objective, 73–74
    Plan Your Job Search Week, 113
    Self-Management Skills, 7–8
    Things My Ideal Job Should Include, 17
    The Top Five Skills My Ideal Jobs Require,
        34–35
    Transferable Skills, 9–11
    What Makes You a Good Worker?, 6
    Your Top Jobs and Industries, 33
writers and editors, 23
yellow pages for cold contacts, 46–47, 142

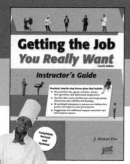

   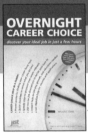